Think Like a Manager

Second Edition

Everything they didn't tell you when they promoted you!

By
Roger Fritz, Ph.D.

Think Like a Manager

Second Edition

Everything they didn't tell you when they promoted you!

By
Roger Fritz, Ph.D.

CAREER PRESS
180 Fifth Avenue
P.O. Box 34
Hawthorne, NJ 07507
1-800-CAREER-1
201-427-0229 (outside U.S.)
FAX: 201-427-2037

THINK LIKE A MANAGER (SECOND EDITION)
EVERTHING THEY DIDN'T TELL YOU WHEN THEY PROMOTED YOU!
ISBN 1-56414-102-0, $16.95
Cover design by A Good Thing, Inc.
Printed in the U.S.A. by Book-mart Press

To order this title by mail, please include price as noted above, $2.50
handling per order, and $1.00 for each book ordered. Send to: Career
Press, Inc., 180 Fifth Ave., P.O. Box 34, Hawthorne, NJ 07507

Or call toll-free 1-800-CAREER-1 (Canada: 201-427-0229) to order
using VISA or MasterCard, or for further information on books from
Career Press.

Library of Congress Cataloging-in-Publication Data

Fritz, Roger.
    Think like a manager : everything they didn't tell you when they
promoted you! / by Roger Fritz. -- 2nd ed.
        p. cm.
    Includes index.
    ISBN 1-56414-102-0 : $16.95
    1. Management. 2. Leadership. 3. Executive ability. I. Title.
HD31.F76 1993
658.4--dc20   93-22765

What Is a Business User's Manual?

It's a one-of-a-kind resource filled with practical tools, checklists, self-tests, guidelines, etc., designed to make your job easier – and your career more successful. Features of the Business User's Manual include:

- Concise, action-oriented explanations of key concepts

- Self-tests, personal assessment worksheets and detailed analyses to help you identify strengths to build on and weaknesses to improve on

- Margin notes that draw your attention to critical management issues – tidbits of fact and business trivia you'll use and enjoy

- Action pages, worksheets, tables, logs – tools you can use to be more productive ... more effective ... more successful

- Legend symbols that guide you through the book ... lead you right where you need to go

What the Experts Have to Say ...

"If there's one skill I'd like to develop in every employee, it's the ability to 'Think Like a Manager.' Roger Fritz has made it possible with this book. Well done."

Kit Grant
President, Learning Dynamics (Canada)

"A self-study format, easy-to-read text, real-world issues and a host of worksheets and checklists. What more could you ask for?"

Sally Jenkins
Author, *Becoming a Promotable Woman*

"'*Think Like a Manager*' has pulled all the keys of effective management into one self-study volume. This is must reading for every supervisor and manager."

Jim Cairo
President, Arena Communications

"Impact! That's the best word to describe what '*Think Like a Manager*' means to me."

Jim Page
Data Manager – Boeing Project
Rockwell International

Other Books Authored By Roger Fritz:

PRACTICAL MANAGEMENT BY OBJECTIVES

PERFORMANCE-BASED MANAGEMENT

PRODUCTIVITY AND RESULTS

RATE YOURSELF AS A MANAGER

YOU'RE IN CHARGE: A Guide for Business and Personal Success

PERSONAL PERFORMANCE CONTRACTS: The Key to Job Success

WHAT MANAGERS NEED TO KNOW

IF THEY CAN — YOU CAN!
   Lessons from America's New Breed of Successful Entrepreneurs

MANAGEMENT IDEAS THAT WORK

FAMILY TIES...AND BINDS:
   How to Solve the Inevitable Problems of Family Businesses

Audiocassettes:

THE INSIDE ADVANTAGE:
   A Self-Paced Program to Make Managers More Effective–
   6 Cassettes-Workbook-Leader's Guide

HOW TO BUILD A WINNING TEAM– 4 Cassettes

Dedication

For Kate
Who thinks like, acts like and is the manager I need.

For my sister Becky
Who taught me not to flinch.

Acknowledgements

This book evolved over many years. Its final publication came about after:

- Bob Burns, my mentor, taught me that managing is a distinctively different type of work.
- My daughter Nancy painstakingly blended core materials with cases and exercises.
- Pat Williamson skillfully typed several versions of the manuscript.

I am indebted to each of them and know they join me in hoping you find it useful.

Roger Fritz

_C_ONTENTS

Chapter 1 – The Professional Manager 1

Chapter 2 – Time Management 37

Chapter 3 – Planning 69

Chapter 4 – Performance-Based Management– PBM 83

Chapter 5 – How to Gain and Retain Good People 123

Chapter 6 – Delegation 146

Chapter 7– Improving Performance 157

Chapter 8– Motivation and Teamwork 195

Chapter 9 – Communication 219

*I*NTRODUCTION

Management Development is Your Responsibility

Management Development is Your Responsibility

Here is an easy-to-understand approach to helping managers help themselves. The material in this workbook is arranged in a carefully planned sequence for use in work sessions or for your private study. It will also provide a practical on-the-job resource for those individuals new to management or for those who need a refresher. Each section includes useful exercises designed to reinforce your learning.

Whatever your management job may be, this book can help you. You will learn:

—The key elements of management.

—What top management should expect.

—How skills must change.

—What effective managers do.

—How to hire and develop the best people.

—Who determines key results.

—How to establish workable goals.

—When problems can lead to growth.

—How to be a better judge of your own progress.

—Manage your career more effectively.

Even if you're a new supervisor, it will help you:

—Evaluate your strengths and weaknesses.

—Determine how they affect your work habits.

—Schedule your time.

—Set priorities.

—Analyze your communication effectiveness.

—Test your skill in making decisions.

—Become proactive.

—Measure your performance objectively.

—Move from task-thinking to performance-thinking.

Management development is your responsibility. In this book you will concentrate on effective management ideas and practices, but more than that, you'll have the opportunity to take a unique look at yourself and your personal development and be challenged to think like a manager.

CHAPTER 1

The Professional Manager

Yesterday's manager was characteristically authoritarian. Today's successful manager is more likely to be a leader who stresses teamwork and cooperative achievement. But before we congratulate ourselves too much, we need to recognize that most present managers also feel they are "managed" by problems of the moment.

What would happen if we could use granddad's magnifying reading glass from "yesterday" and take a close look at today's best management principles and practices? Maybe we could become better managers tomorrow! We know we will be expected to react more quickly, to think more deeply, to understand more clearly, to stimulate more positively, and to set a course more precisely than did our predecessors. So let's look at these basics. Pick up the magnifying glass, turn the page, and focus in...

Systems of Management & Leadership

This chart summarizes how management concepts and systems have evolved in the past 50 years. Note especially that none are recommended at all times and for all situations. All have strengths and limitations. There is no perfect management system.

Evolving Systems of Management & Leadership

ASPECTS	AUTHORITY SYSTEM	Developmental TECHNICAL SYSTEM	INTERACTION SYSTEM	DECISION-MAKING SYSTEM	LEADERSHIP OBJECTIVES SYSTEM
Image of Manager	A Take Charge Type Of Person	Scientific Manager	Interactor & Human Relator	Planner & Decision Maker	Professional Manager & Leader
World of	Organization Chart, Policy Procedures	Principles & Fundamentals Methods	Individual & Group Relations	Alternatives & Probabilities	Internal & External Forces
Language Approach	POIM: Plan, Organize, Initi-ate, Measure	Standard Operating Procedure	Relations, Inter-relations, Inter-dependency	Quantitative Decision Rules	Plans of Action Objectives & Results
Organiza-tion Focus	Carry Out Policies & Orders	Primary Production Unit	Formal Informal Groups	Logic & Variables System	Balanced Cooperative Trusteeship
Mood & Manner	Structured & Authoritarian	Austere & Imposed	Permissive & Clinical	Ordered & Programmed	Plans & Performance
Emphasis & Focus	Chain of Com-mand, Channels Performance	Work Flows & Efficiency Measures	Interactive Relations & Reactions	Logical, Rational Relationships	Autonomy with Accountability
Progress Review Procedure	A Trait-Based Administra-tive Club	A Form Process, Procedure	An Interpersonal Interchange	A Technical Review	A Fact-Based Analytical Tool
At Worst It Can Be	Controlling, Directive, Coercive	Bloodless, Mechanical, Instrumented	Evaluative, Pathological, Clinical	Abstract, Impersonal, Non-Human	Conforming, Controlling, Manipulative
At Best It Can Provide	Order, Direction, Progress	Partial View of Management & Operations	Personal Interpersonal Behavioral	Logical Interaction Decision	Cooperation Teamwork, Achievement

If we have reached a time when management can be practiced as a profession, what are the basic qualifications? Are traditional credentials trustworthy (college degrees — certification exams — seniority or years of experience)? Or are informal measures more reliable (personal contacts — trust — "clout")?

What do you consider to be the basic qualifications of managers? How would you define a professional manager? Rank yourself on the Professional Manager checklist on the next page.

We will concentrate on each point in this outline as we move through the book.

> *"As I grow older, I pay less attention to what men say. I just watch what they do."*
> Andrew Carnegie

Rank Yourself on the
Professional Manager Checklist

The Professional Manager:

1. IS COMMITTED TO
   ☐ Self-Development ☐ Life-Long Learning

2. IS EFFECTIVE IN MANAGING
   ☐ Work ☐ People ☐ Relations ☐ Situations

3. IS SELF-MOTIVATED

4. IS ACCURATE IN ANALYZING
   ☐ Where are we now?
   ☐ What should we drop?
   ☐ How much can we do?
   ☐ What is wrong (NOT who is wrong)?

5. IS REALISTIC & FLEXIBLE REGARDING EXPECTATIONS

6. DISCRIMINATES BETWEEN
   ☐ Activities and Results
   ☐ Efficiency and Effectiveness
   ☐ Tasks and Goals

7. CONTINUOUSLY NEGOTIATES TO DETERMINE
   ☐ Key Result Areas
   ☐ Success Indicators
   ☐ Measures of Progress – Who Will Do What by When?
   ☐ Action Plans

8. COMMUNICATES REGULARLY
   ☐ Up ☐ Down ☐ Across

9. APPRAISES PERFORMANCE OBJECTIVELY

10. BUILDS ON STRENGTHS
   ☐ Personal ☐ Subordinate's ☐ Organization's

Are You a Professional Manager?

Managerial Expectations

One of the keys to becoming a professional, effective manager is being provided (and providing your subordinates) with realistic expectations. To succeed in accomplishing common objectives, individuals must:

1. Be aware of the objectives for their job.

2. Be aware of how they are expected to contribute towards them.

Just as you have expectations of your subordinates, so does upper management have expectations of you. To put your job and expectations in proper perspective, it's a good idea to ask yourself: "If I were responsible for this organization, what would I expect?"

Basically, top management should expect:

1. To have an effective method of defining results expected from managers.

2. To improve the performance of managers continuously.

3. To secure and hold the best recruits.

4. To provide first-class education for tomorrow's job, as well as today's, at lower cost.

5. To have a reliable and objective means of judging the performance of managers.

6. To have a flexible succession plan for staffing the organization in the future.

7. To motivate managers and reward them equitably in line with results achieved.

8. To improve the flow of communication up, down and across the business.

Top Management

> *"There is no future in any job. The future lies in the person who holds the job."*
> G.W. Grave

Are there other expectations you would include? List them below. Why are they important?

EXPECTATIONS	WHY IMPORTANT
1._____	a. _____
	b. _____
	c. _____
	d. _____
2._____	a. _____
	b. _____
	c. _____
	d. _____
3. _____	a. _____
	b. _____
	c. _____
	d. _____
4. _____	a. _____
	b. _____
	c. _____
	d. _____
5. _____	a. _____
	b. _____
	c. _____
	d _____.

Test Your Assumptions

All of us bring our personal values and standards to our job. They play a critical part in determining our expectations of other people and their work. By recognizing these values and assumptions, we can better understand why we fail (or succeed) in meeting expectations. This quiz will test your assumptions and help you discover your own style of management.

Test your assumptions regarding people, their work and how to get people to do the work that is expected. Complete the test by checking the appropriate column for each of the 15 statements before reading the explanation that follows the exercise. Two simple ground rules should be followed in completing the test:

1. Read each statement and immediately place a check in one of the four columns. Your assumptions are being measured here, not your carefully reasoned response. Therefore, answer at once, not after making qualifications of the statements or by seeking the "right" answer. In this test, there are no right or wrong answers. There are only your answers. The best answer describes what you actually believe. Any other answer will only cloud the picture we are looking for — your instinctive pattern of behavior.

2. Think of "people" in this exercise in a rather general sense. Don't think of specific individuals, either "strong right arms" or "constant thorns in the side." We are looking for your general pattern of behavior, the image you project to others.

Now answer these questions by checking the column for each statement that comes closest to your position. The test should take no more than three or four minutes. (The original use of masculine pronouns has not been altered because of the author's desire to keep the current language consistent with the language used to generate historical statistical results.)

Test Your Assumptions Regarding People and Their Work

Managerial Assessment Quiz

(Check One)	Strongly Disagree	Disagree	Agree	Strongly Agree
1. Almost anyone could probably improve job performance quite a bit if he really wanted to.	___	___	___	___
2. It is unrealistic to expect people to show the same enthusiasm for their work as for their leisure activities.	___	___	___	___
3. Even when given encouragement by the boss, very few people show the desire to improve themselves on the job.	___	___	___	___
4. If you give people enough money, they are less likely to worry about such intangibles as status or recognition.	___	___	___	___
5. Usually when people talk about wanting more responsible jobs, they really mean they want more money and status.	___	___	___	___
6. Because most people don't like to make decisions on their own, it is hard to get them to assume responsibility.	___	___	___	___
7. Being tough with people will usually get them to do what you want.	___	___	___	___
8. A good way to get people to do more work is to crack down on them once in a while.	___	___	___	___
9. It weakens a person's prestige whenever he has to admit that a subordinate was right and he was wrong.	___	___	___	___

(Check One)

	Strongly Disagree	Disagree	Agree	Strongly Agree
10. The most effective supervisor is one who gets the results expected, regardless of the methods used in handling people.	____	____	____	____
11. It is too much to expect that people will try to do a good job without being prodded by their boss.	____	____	____	____
12. The boss who expects people to set their own standards for superior performance will probably find they don't set them very high.	____	____	____	____
13. If people don't use much imagination and ingenuity on the job, it is probably because relatively few people have much of either.	____	____	____	____
14. One problem in asking for the ideas of subordinates is that their perspective is too limited for their suggestions to be of much practical value.	____	____	____	____
15. It is only human nature for people to try to do as little work as they can get away with.	____	____	____	____
A. Totals for Columns	____	____	____	____
B. Above Totals	1x____	2x____	3x____	x4____

C. GRAND TOTAL   _____

For scoring and assessment follow on to the next page.

Scoring and Meaning of the Test

1. Total the number of check marks in each column and place these numbers in the appropriate blanks at the end of the exercise. If you have not skipped any statements, and if you have totaled correctly, the **Totals for Columns** row should add up to 15.

2. Next you should multiply whatever total you have for each column as follows: multiply your total in the **Strongly Disagree** column by 1 and write this figure below column 1; multiply your total in the next column by 2 and write this figure below column 2; multiply the third column's answer by 3 and the fourth column's answer by 4 in the same manner.

3. Now add up the four sums. The sum of these four figures is your **Grand Total.** Again, if you have not made any mathematical errors, your answer is somewhere between 15 and 60.

In order to interpret your numerical score, record it between 15 and 60 on the figure below and circle it.

Managerial Styles — Where Are You?

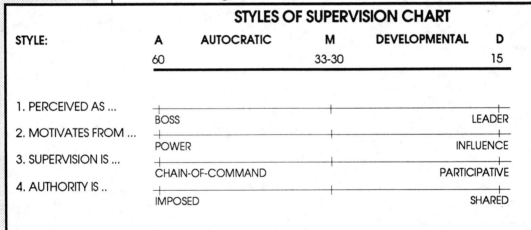

STYLES OF SUPERVISION CHART

STYLE:	A	AUTOCRATIC	M	DEVELOPMENTAL	D
	60		33-30		15

1. PERCEIVED AS ...	BOSS	LEADER
2. MOTIVATES FROM ...	POWER	INFLUENCE
3. SUPERVISION IS ...	CHAIN-OF-COMMAND	PARTICIPATIVE
4. AUTHORITY IS ..	IMPOSED	SHARED

The line A to D is intended to provide for all possible sets of assumptions regarding people and their work. Points A to M represent various degrees of autocratic or authoritarian styles of management, while M to D cover differing degrees of democratic or developmental supervision styles. Were you surprised by your score?

The theory here is that your set of assumptions about people and their work leads you to develop a certain style of management. The autocrat thinks that people have little ambition, try to avoid responsibility and want to be told what to do at all times. This leads the manager to assume the responsibility for setting objectives and to exercise close control to see that these objectives are carried out. It fosters a relationship in which subordinates are quite dependent, showing relatively little self-expression or self-responsibility. In this sort of climate, participative decision-making finds little nourishment.

On the other hand, developmental supervision challenges people with real opportunity and encourages them to excellent performance. It looks upon people as accepting and even enjoying their work and eager to accept responsibility. It leads to participation in the setting of objectives and to the exercise of broad control that allows people to grow by monitoring themselves. It fosters a relationship in which subordinates can be quite independent and self-reliant if their temperaments allow.

Notice how the actions of the individual manager will flow logically from attitudes or assumptions about people and their capacity for development. The autocrat believes people dislike work and avoid it when they can; therefore, they must be closely directed and controlled.

The Autocratic Manager:

1. Says little unless something is wrong.
2. Usually is not interested in the ideas of others.
3. Decides what information people need.
4. Changes demands unexpectedly.
5. Is sometimes hard to talk to.
6. Discourages people from taking risks.
7. Sets objectives for subordinates.
8. Personally determines performance standards.

Conversely, the developmental manager believes that people enjoy work and can direct and control themselves. People accept and seek responsibility for their actions.

The Developmental Manager:

1. Considers ideas that conflict with his/her own.
2. Allows a reasonable margin for error.
3. Tries to help others learn from their mistakes.
4. Has consistently high expectations.
5. Encourages people to reach in new directions.
6. Helps people understand the objectives of their jobs.
7. Allows people to make their own commitments.
8. Sets objectives with people.

It is rare to find one or the other style of management in the pure state. Managers usually fall somewhere along a line from the pure autocrat on the one hand to the pure developmental manager on the other. The individual circumstances surrounding any action may dictate what you will do at any given moment, but the general pattern of behavior you develop over time is what will place you somewhere on the continuum.

Many groups have taken this test, providing sufficient information to check its validity and reliability. According to those who devised it, your score probably indicates something like the following: If you scored 39 or higher, you are probably somewhat autocratic. If you scored 29 or less, you are probably somewhat developmental. If you scored between 29 and 39, you don't have strong leanings one way or the other, and we don't know what you'll do.

Does your score agree with where you guessed your position might be on the scale? If you would have placed yourself on the "wrong" side of center, you may be in trouble — you may not know enough about your own method of handling people, or at least don't have the same image of yourself as others do. The score on this test is probably the view others have of you.

If you are way out at the autocratic end of the scale (between 52 and 60), then you may have trouble by tending to be high-handed in dealing with people. You apparently feel that people do not have much initiative of their own, that they have to be watched very carefully, that they have nothing to contribute of value to a group endeavor, that they are motivated primarily by selfishness. You are probably, therefore, likely to be too control-oriented in directing their activities and will likely run into difficulty getting people to take initiative because of their fear of failure.

Here are words typically used to describe people on the autocratic side of the scale:

- **Domineering**
- **Manipulating**
- **Intimidating**
- **Competitive**
- **Blunt**
- **Harsh**
- **Critical**
- **Decisive**
- **Direct**
- **Self-reliant**

If you are way out on the developmental end of the scale (that is, scored somewhere between 15 and 20), chances are you are also in trouble. This is because you apparently do not have sufficient sense of the need for controls. You are perhaps too permissive in your approach to people and might well be living in the proverbial dream world of the naive idealist. You may tend to refrain from holding people accountable for achieving the standards agreed upon.

Here are words typically used to describe people on the developmental side of the scale:

- **Supporting**
- **Flexible**
- **Analytical**
- **Understanding**
- **Stable**
- **Trusting**
- **Implementor**
- **Planner**
- **Approachable**
- **Tolerant**

If you scored a middle score (that is, 30 to 33 or thereabouts), you could also be in trouble. It depends on how you got this score. If you checked some answers in the first column and some answers in the last column, so that the pluses offset the minuses, then you are probably in trouble, because you do not recognize the inconsistency of your responses. A careful reading of the 15 statements will indicate that all of them really say the same thing in a different way. So at the very least, you should not strongly agree with some and then strongly disagree with others. Answers running down the

Autocratic People

Developmental People

13

middle two columns, even though they are labeled "agree" and "disagree" are really not inconsistent, given the rapidity of your response and the absence of a neutral position.

In-Between People

Here are words typically used to describe people in the middle of the scale:

- **Experimenter**
- **Cautious**
- **Avoiding**
- **Evaluator**
- **Accepting**

- **Indecisive**
- **Appeasing**
- **Analyzer**
- **Patient**
- **Accommodating**

Now look at these words and ask yourself if it is possible to overuse them. If so, what words would you use to describe the consequences of overuse? For example:

- **Critical behavior** – if overused may cause – feeling of inferiority
- **Analytical behavior** – if overused may cause – excessive delays
- **Indecisiveness** – if overused may cause – loss to competitor

Have you found your place on the Styles of Supervision chart? On the next page, you'll find another way to determine, in a preliminary way at least, how others may be evaluating your leadership style.

> *"A successful executive in business is one who can delegate all the responsibility, shift all the blame, and appropriate all the credit."*

To assist further in your self-evaluation of your tendencies or style as a manager, consider the questions raised following this chart.

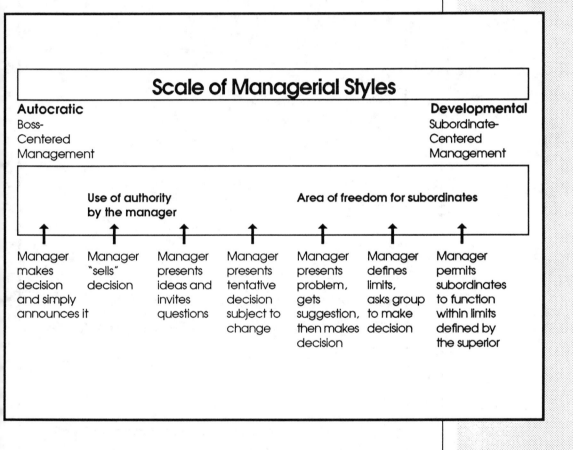

Scale of Managerial Styles

Autocratic
Boss-
Centered
Management

Developmental
Subordinate-
Centered
Management

Use of authority by the manager

Area of freedom for subordinates

| Manager makes decision and simply announces it | Manager "sells" decision | Manager presents ideas and invites questions | Manager presents tentative decision subject to change | Manager presents problem, gets suggestion, then makes decision | Manager defines limits, asks group to make decision | Manager permits subordinates to function within limits defined by the superior |

Worksheet

In the space below indicate when you believe a Boss-Centered, Autocratic Managerial Style is appropriate.

Tasks

Example – limited time available

Situations

Example – emergencies

Time

Example – if delay would be costly

Personalities

Example – people who prefer to have their boss decide

What are the advantages of the Boss-Centered Style?

Example – quick action

What are the disadvantages or limitations of the Boss-Centered Style?

Example – limits initiative of other people

Worksheet

In the space below indicate when you believe a Subordinate-Centered, Developmental Managerial Style is appropriate.

Tasks

Example – complex problem, no easy solution

Situations

Example – many ideas needed

Time

Example – pacing and scheduling are possible

Personalities

Example – variety, but have in common a desire to be accountable

What are the advantages of the Subordinate-Centered Style?

Example – more thorough examination of issues

What are the disadvantages of the Subordinate-Centered Style?

Example – "analysis paralysis"

"When all is said and done, your value to others depends on only one thing — how much they need you."

See Yourself as Others See You

Have you found your place on the Styles of Supervision Chart?
Do you feel fairly confident that this is truly your managerial
style? It is quite possible that the way you perceive your style and
the way your subordinates see you are considerably different!
Below you will find another way to determine, in a preliminary
way at least, how others may be evaluating your leadership style.

Yes No

1. I believe in accepting my subordinates'
   ideas even when they differ from my own.   ____ ____

2. I believe that my instructions or procedures
   should always be followed as issued.   ____ ____

3. I usually try to get the support of people
   working for me before I proceed with an
   important policy change.   ____ ____

4. People in authority should present the image
   of authority in the way they dress, communicate and conduct themselves.   ____ ____

5. It's best to let your people implement your
   instructions the way they think best.   ____ ____

6. I believe that my subordinates need to be
   ruled with an iron fist. It gives them the
   direction and guidance they need.   ____ ____

7. I treat my subordinates as my equals.   ____ ____

8. The suggestions I receive from subordinates
   are rarely very good since these people don't
   have the range of experience necessary to see
   the picture as I do.   ____ ____

9. I rarely change the duties of persons reporting
   to me without first talking it over with them.   ____ ____

10. Good managers give their subordinates complete,
    detailed instructions of how things should be done
    to get them done correctly.   ____ ____

11. I accept suggestions from people in my unit, and I very often use their ideas. ____ ____

12. Consulting subordinates in important decisions is a time-waster — especially if you want results. ____ ____

13. One of the best ways to manage is to have regular staff meetings where you solicit ideas. ____ ____

14. To cut down on time loss and frustration, I often do things my way. They get done faster, better, and with greater efficiency that way. ____ ____

Don't be discouraged if your own and your subordinates' perceptions of your style don't match. Realizing that the two perceptions may differ is the first step toward improving your managerial behavior "What we are" isn't necessarily a permanent condition. The dream of "WHAT WE CAN BE" encourages us to look for Keys to Effective Leadership.

> *"Perhaps the most important lesson — the professional manager is a servant. Rank does not confer privilege or give power. It imposes responsibility."*
> Peter Drucker

19

Keys to Effective Leadership

Research shows that we are capable of moving our own leadership style closer to the ideal by:

1. Developing a work climate that encourages trust, candor and open communication with a free sharing of work-related information.

2. Adopting the belief that the best motivation is self-motivation and that if the proper climate and leadership are provided, most employees will want to be productive and efficient.

3. Involving employees in problem-solving and improvement-planning when they are in a position to make a contribution.

4. Listening to employees and trying to see merit in their needs.

5. Setting clear goals and helping employees understand organizational objectives.

6. Rearranging jobs to allow a greater degree of responsibility and self-direction.

7. Recognizing that conflicts between the needs of individuals and the organization are inevitable, but should be confronted openly using problem-solving strategies.

8. Using mistakes as a learning opportunity rather than concentrating on placing blame.

9. Having high expectations of others while providing them support and encouragement in attaining their objectives.

10. Providing recognition for superior performance.

Dr. Robert K. Burns, Founding Director of the Industrial Relations Center at the University of Chicago, spent a lifetime sorting out the essential aspects of managerial functions and developing tools to deal with them. Here is his breakdown of the five areas that must be managed to manage effectively.

Check those aspects within each area that you believe are not being dealt with adequately in your area of responsibility. These are needs for which action plans should be developed.

Professional Management —
Concepts, Techniques, Skills, Applications

"What Must Be Managed — To Manage Effectively"

AREA I – MANAGING SELF (The Introspective Framework)
- **Self-Appraisal Before Judging Others**
- **Analysis of Personal Behavioral Style**

1. Self-Discovery – The Key to Constructive Action
2. Objective Analysis – To Yield Better Decisions Than Instinct
3. Evaluation as a Role Model – Pattern of Exemplary Leadership
4. Effectiveness as a Teacher – To Practice What is Taught
5. Accountable Behavior – To Initiate Action and Assure Results

AREA II – MANAGING WORK (The Results Framework)
- **Strategic Plans, Priorities, Posterities**
- **Managing by Objectives and Results (MOR)**

1. Role and Mission – Key Areas/Priorities for Results Clarification, Consensus, Commitment
2. Objectives and Results – To be Accomplished in Priority Areas – What, Where, When
3. Plans of Action – To Accomplish Them – Schedules, Assignments, Communication
4. Progress Review – Of the Vital Signs to Improve Work and Develop Staff
5. Relating Managerial Objectives – To Budgeting and Financial Objectives

AREA III – MANAGING PEOPLE (The Personnel Framework)
- **Staffing and Strengthening the Organization**
- **Training, Performance and Development**

1. Recruitment and Selection – From Inside and Outside the Organization

Functional Accountability Area I

Functional Accountability Area II

Functional Accountability Area III

2. Induction and On-The-Job Training – To Meet Work Requirements

3. Discipline Without Punishment – Using Work Objectives and Natural Consequences

4. Performance and Potential – Their Assessment, Improvement, Development

5. Managerial Reserves and Replacements – Who Are Ready, Qualified, Available

AREA IV – MANAGING RELATIONS (The Interpersonal Framework)

- **Communicating with Individuals and Groups**
- **Increasing Motivation, Cooperation, and Teamwork**

1. Climate-Setting Processes – For Developing Trust and Teamwork

2. Building Supportive Relationships – Colleague-Helper vs. Critic-Judge

3. Effective Communication Techniques – Questioning, Listening, Responding

4. Basic Motivation – Methods for Its Modification and Mobilization

5. Coaching and Counseling – On Work-Related Problems

AREA V – MANAGING SITUATIONS (The Interaction Framework)

- **Handling Situations and Behaviors**
- **Problem-Solving and Decision-Making**

1. Analyzing and Handling Situations – Cause-Reaction/Ends-Means Analyses

2. Changing Attitudes and Behaviors – Of Individuals and Groups

3. Constructive Confrontation – Using I Selectively and Effectively

4. Reducing and Resolving Conflict – Methods That Work and Those That Fail

5. Sharing, Stating and Solving Problems – Processes, Techniques, Skills, Applications

Personal Accountability Area IV

Personal Accountability Area V

Rate Your Supervisor

Observation is one of the ways by which we learn; children learn by observing their parents, adolescents learn by observing their peers, and subordinates learn by observing their bosses. Under the best circumstances, supervisors can provide us with career growth as well as personal counseling and coaching. Even competent people need all the help they can get. Ongoing support from the boss is a key factor. Here is a quick quiz to evaluate your supervisor.

Score each element from 0 (poor) to 10 (excellent)

My Supervisor Is:

1...informative. Quick to let me in on information that might be useful to me or stimulating or of long-term professional interest. _____

2...objective. Negotiates goals — determines priorities — monitors progress. Knows the apparently important from the truly important. _____

3...effective. Teaches me to learn from my mistakes as he/she does. _____

4...decisive. Determined to get at those decisions that can tie up organizations for days. _____

5...available. If I have a problem I can't solve. But forceful in making me do my best to bring in solutions, not problems. _____

6...fair. Concerned about me and how I'm doing. Gives credit where credit is due, but holds me to my commitments. _____

7...tough. Won't waste time. Is more jealous of subordinate's time than his/her own. _____

8...patient. Knows when to bite the bullet until I solve my own problem. _____

9...humble. Admits own mistakes openly — learns from them and expects subordinates to do the same. _____

10...humorous. Appreciates the lighter side of situations. Laughs even harder when the joke's on him/her. _____

TOTAL _____

Supervisor Rating

Would you be comfortable discussing your ratings with your boss? If not, why not? If yes, when will you do it?

> *"There are many paths to success, but the route to failure is clear — try to please everyone!"*

How do you think your subordinates would rate you on these 10 points?

Even though your current boss may not rate high on this quiz, the important factor is how you rate on these ten points. Take the quiz again, but this time place yourself in your subordinates' shoes and rate yourself, or better yet ask them to rate you.

If your score is:

90 – 100	Pat yourself on the back!
75 – 89	Good work climate
65 – 74	Likely subordinate friction/resentment
50 – 64	Definitely needs improvement
Below 50	Headed for trouble, but don't be discouraged; this workbook is designed to help you.

Start to work where it is needed most!

There are other questions to ask yourself and your subordinates about your effectiveness as a leader.

Continuing to look at yourself objectively —

How Do You Rate as a Leader?

Do You: Usually Rarely

1. Encourage participation by others?   ____   ____
   Recent good example:

   Recent bad example:

2. Have realistic goals?   ____   ____
   Recent good example:

   Recent bad example:

3. Question yourself?   ____   ____
   Recent good example:

   Recent bad example

4. Have awareness of group
   dynamics and loyalties?   ____   ____
   Recent good example:

   Recent bad example:

5. Become a part of the group
   before initiating action?   ____   ____
   Recent good example:

   Recent bad example:

6. Compete fairly?   ____   ____
   Recent good example:

   Recent bad example:

> **What's Your Leadership Quotient?**

	Usually	Rarely

7. Have high frustration tolerance? _____ _____
   Recent good example:

   Recent bad example:

8. Win without gloating? _____ _____
   Recent good example:

   Recent bad example:

9. Lose without pouting? _____ _____
   Recent good example:

   Recent bad example:

10. Control the impulse to "get even"? _____ _____
    Recent good example:

    Recent bad example:

11. Stay alert for restrictions? _____ _____
    Recent good example:

    Recent bad example:

If you answered "usually" to most of these questions, you are probably a developmental leader, and your work group is "primed" for success if the people in it want to be accountable for their actions.

If you answered "rarely" to most of these questions, you are likely to be so ego-driven that you will have difficulty sustaining support over time.

Choose the area that most needs improvement and concentrate on it.

Identifying Successful First-Line Supervisors

Who is a successful supervisor? Here are four basic attributes.

Motivated mainly by achievement, successful supervisors accept reality. They "push" harder than their employees like, but they also "pull," which makes the pressure more acceptable. They establish the way to get things done and let everyone know what the goals are. They are not satisfied merely to delegate tasks and responsibilities; they may by-pass their assistants and check details personally. They have self-confidence, but constantly worry about falling short of the objective. Achievement is their main concern, and they are respected (although not loved) by their employees for that. Some subordinates regard such supervisors as harsh taskmasters. They are!

How do you measure up? My self-rating (circle one):

1	2	3	4	5	6	7	8	9	10
poor				average					excellent

Successful supervisors support higher authority in working toward company goals. Once decisions are made, they accept the decisions of higher management. They regard higher authority as being more experienced, more knowledgeable, and more likely to recommend the most effective course of action — even when opinions differ.

How do you measure up? My self-rating (circle one):

1	2	3	4	5	6	7	8	9	10
poor				average					excellent

Successful supervisors anticipate most of the consequences of their decisions — what will happen next week or next month as a result of plans and decisions. They operate with confidence.

Successful supervisors combine and arrange so that they know what is expected. Because they anticipate problems and systematically plan the work, subordinates know that the supervisor is aware of what is going on and act accordingly.

How do you measure up? My self-rating (circle one):

1	2	3	4	5	6	7	8	9	10
poor				average					excellent

Desire for Achievement

Attitude Toward Authority

Ability to Organize

Successful supervisors are often dissatisfied with their own performances: If they hadn't done this or that or had done this or that better, the results would have been more satisfying. He or she is a person with an itch to do better.

The employees must be convinced that their supervisor knows what he or she is doing and has their interest at heart. When a request is refused, a logical explanation is given. It may not be persuasive, but it is reasonable. Explanations are willingly made as to why rules are to be followed. Mutually acceptable answers will be found to work-related problems. The successful supervisor insists that the job be well done, and on time, and clearly is not soft-hearted about employees. He or she gets respect from employees by influence, not by formal authority.

How do you measure up? My self-rating (circle one)

1	2	3	4	5	6	7	8	9	10
poor				average					excellent

How Skills Must Change

After you and your organization have determined who the successful supervisors are, you must now develop their skills toward more progressively responsible managerial positions.

The following chart clearly illustrates how skills must change, as managerial levels do.

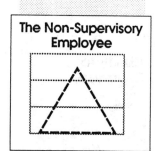

The Non-Supervisory Employee

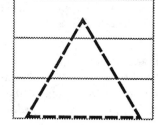

Conceptual Skill

Human Relations Skill

Technical Skill

EXPECTATIONS:

- Excellent technical or production skills.
- Acceptable skills in dealing with fellow employees.
- Minimal requirements for planning/looking ahead.

The First-Line Supervisor

Conceptual Skill

Human Relations Skill

Technical Skill

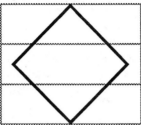

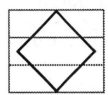

The First-Line
Supervisor

EXPECTATIONS:

- Less technical/production skills required.
- Human relations skills are most important.
- Planning skills increased significantly.

Middle Manager

Conceptual Skill

Human Relations Skill

Technical Skill

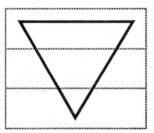

Middle Manager

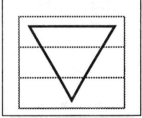

EXPECTATIONS:

- Most technical/production skills are delegated to others.
- Must communicate effectively up, down and across the organization.
- Anticipating problems and evaluating options is critical.

The Top Management Executive

Conceptual Skill

Human Relations Skill

Technical Skill

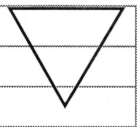

The Top Manage-
ment Executive

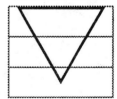

EXPECTATIONS:

- Technical/production skills needed least.
- Must set the climate for effective interpersonal relationships.
- Planning for the future is the top priority.

Organization Development

Critical to the success of an organization and its managers is the opportunity for growth, both personal and professional. The only way for individuals to progress up the managerial ladder is through continuous and effective development. Each of us wants to be related to an effective organization that can offer us opportunity. What specifics are involved in developing an organization to its maximum potential?

Organization Development is a continuing process of self-improvement, a self-correcting means for organizations to change and improve. It involves:

- Confronting the problems that slow down the organization.
- Getting decisions made at the level where the facts are.
- Developing effective teamwork.
- Dealing with conflicts openly and constructively.
- Increasing awareness of how process affects performance.
- Gaining support by senior management.
- Providing each manager and potential manager with challenges and opportunities for maximum self-development on present jobs and for advancement.
- Offering support to the entire management group towards the improvement of skills and competence as a future investment.
- Providing managers for the organization in sufficient numbers and diversity to meet the needs of the years ahead.
- Devising effective systems to make it easier for managers to carry out manager development responsibilities

---

"It's not the most intellectual job in the world, but I do have to know the letters."
Vanna White

The Development Process

Is:

- Identifying capable people.
- Testing them under fire.
- Decision-making in increasingly difficult situations.
- Managing more people in higher positions.
- Developing confidence.
- Judgment based upon performance.
- Reward for taking responsibility.
- Opportunity for upward mobility.
- Responsibility at the lowest competent level.
- Guidance based on future performance.
- Based upon demonstrated success.

Is Not:

- Directly related to credentials.
- Undertaken *for* someone but *with* them.
- A social responsibility to underachievers.
- A classroom or textbook educational process.
- "Educating" as a substitute for "doing."
- A training program.
- A single technique.
- Sloughing off counseling responsibility.
- Eliminating mistakes.
- Placing blame.
- A self-fulfilling prophecy.

Development, Training or Education?

If you're wondering what type of development is necessary in your unit, by answering the following questions you can —

Assess Your Organizational Needs

Answer each question related to your present position:

1. What does it take to be a good performer in this area?

2. What would you identify as key elements of successful performance if you were orienting a new employee in this position?

3. What are the major elements of this job that need to be improved?

4. What processes are not effectively being used?

5. What are the consequences of current problem areas/poor performance areas?

6. What would you like to see improved in the performance of persons in this department?

7. Are there any organizational policies/practices that hinder good performance?

8. Is poor performance influenced by the organizational structure?

9. What can the organization do to make your job easier?

Summary:
Plans for Development of Individuals

Professional managers are developed. Very few are "naturals." This chapter has provided many guides for self-direction, because each manager has a dual responsibility — first for personal self-development, and second for creating the best managerial climate to stimulate the development of those people for whom he/she is directly responsible. The policy must, of course, be supported by techniques and methods of high professional quality. Here is a summary of the key factors involved in developing and retaining professional managers. How does your organization rate?

	My organization's rating:		
We have:	**Poor**	**Fair**	**Excellent**
1. A sound organizational structure.	_____	_____	_____
2. Management job descriptions focused on results and management performance standards.	_____	_____	_____
3. Short-term priority plans that integrate with the organization's overall plans.	_____	_____	_____
4. Results expected that are clearly defined with advanced methods of performance review.	_____	_____	_____
5. Management training for the individual and for groups, within and outside the organization.	_____	_____	_____
6. A management succession plan so that we can promote well-qualified people from within.	_____	_____	_____
7. An equitable, competitive salary structure.	_____	_____	_____
8. Modern techniques of recruitment and selection.	_____	_____	_____

> *"The worst part of me — the most boring part — is my guilt complex. I feel almost responsible for the fall of Adam and Eve."*
> Laurence Olivier

	Poor	Fair	Excellent
9. Goals and plans of the organization that are clearly understood and used as the basis for everyday work.	_____	_____	_____
10. Necessary information for decision-making that moves through all levels of the organization.	_____	_____	_____
11. Clear interrelationships among jobs.	_____	_____	_____
12. Opportunities within the organization to allow individuals to develop to their fullest potential.	_____	_____	_____

Now, examine your answers. Use the space below to write your comments. Wherever you checked poor or fair, ask yourself — Why do I feel this way? What is the evidence? What are the consequences? Whom should I talk to about this?

Question #_____

- Why do I feel this way?

- What is the evidence?

- What are the consequences?

- Whom should I talk to about this?

Questions for Personal Development

1. What is the major emphasis of this chapter?

2. What do you feel are the most important things you
learned from this chapter?
1)

2)

3)

3. How can you apply what you learned to your current job?
1)

2)

3)

4. What objectives will you set to improve? By when (date)?
1)

2)

3)

5. Who can help you most in applying what you learned in
this chapter?

6. What are the major roadblocks you expect that may hinder
your progress in applying what you learned in this chapter?
Roadblock   **Why?**
1)

2)

3)

7. How will you communicate the most important points in
this chapter to your key people?

8. What preparation is necessary for this introduction?

9. What changes do you expect to make that will achieve greater motivation of your team?

Change   **By when – date?**

1)

2)

3)

10. How will you monitor to assure that performance has improved, i.e., productivity has increased? (Reports, meetings, etc.)

11. What work-related problems concern you most in evaluating how you will benefit from this chapter?

12. Once you've accomplished several milestones, how will you continue developing new ideas and objectives related to this chapter?

13. How would you summarize the change you expect to see in yourself one year from now as a result of what you learned in this chapter?

CHAPTER 2

Time Management

Does this poem speak for you some days?
"If I Could Just Get Organized"

There may be nothing wrong with you, the way you live,
the work you do,
  But I can very plainly see exactly what is wrong with me.

It isn't that I'm indolent or dodging duty by intent;
  I work as hard as anyone, and yet I get so little done,

The morning goes, the noon is here, before I know, the night
is near,
  And all around me, I regret, are things I haven't finished yet.

If I could just get organized. But here's my trouble right along
  I do the things that don't amount to very much, of no account,

That really seem important though, and let a lot of matters go.
  I nibble this, I nibble that, but never finish what I'm at.

I work as hard as anyone, and yet, I get so little done,
  I'd do so much you'd be surprised, if I could just get organized.

                                        Author Unknown

If this expresses a feeling you have often, this section can be
especially helpful.

An understanding of yourself — your strengths and weaknesses, your habits, your personal patterns and your health — is important for you to make the best use of your time.

Personal Inventory of Strengths and Weaknesses

For each of the following items, give yourself a numerical rating from zero to ten. Here are some guidelines: Give yourself a zero if you have absolutely none of the element mentioned; ten if you have more of it than anyone you have known or worked with. If you think you have about as much as most other people, give yourself a five.

(0-10 points)

1. I am well qualified for my job and the skills it involves. _____

2. I am very persuasive and usually get others to agree with me. _____

3. I get along well with others. _____

4. I am honest, not only with myself but with others. _____

5. I have great powers of concentration; very little distracts me. _____

6. I learn very quickly anything I put my mind to. _____

7. I am a natural leader, always in the center of groups making things happen. _____

8. My health and stamina are excellent; I never feel too tired to do what I have to do. _____

9. I am self-disciplined and do what is required. _____

10. I am decisive, quick and sure in my choices. _____

11. I am well organized. _____

12. I have a great deal of courage and am ready to forge ahead, without letting fear keep me back. _____

13. I am creative, have new ideas and am ready to hear the ideas of others. _____

14. I am able to "catch on fast" and figure out situations quickly. _____

15. I have good judgment and often get hunches that I can follow to successful conclusions. _____

16. Other people recognize my leadership and are willing to follow. _____

17. I work well in a team situation and let others participate in the decision-making. _____

18. I feel within me a great potential for further improvement of my abilities and my personality. _____

19. I am satisfied with my present goals at work and feel comfortable and optimistic about achieving them. _____

20. I have great energy, drive and motivation to achieve my personal goals and feel confident that I am expending my energy wisely in meeting them. _____

TOTAL _____

> *"When I misuse time, I have wasted the only resource I can never restore."*

How Did You Do?

 Items rated less than five will detract seriously from your effectiveness as a manager.

 Items rated seven and above should serve you well as a manager.

Work Influenced by Personal Strengths and Weaknesses

Use the forms provided on the next pages to list four of your personal strengths and weaknesses from those you discovered in the previous exercise. For each strength, list several parts of your work that benefit from your use of this ability. For each weakness, list any parts of your job that might be suffering as a result of this weakness. Also, note under each weakness what you think or feel you can do to improve yourself, and set up a date some time in the future to evaluate yourself again and to note any progress you have made at overcoming each weakness.

Personal Strength	Work Influenced by This Strength
1.	a. b. c. d.
2.	a. b. c. d.
3.	a. b. c. d.
4.	a. b. c. d.

Personal Weakness	Work Influenced by This Weakness	Steps to Take to Overcome This Weakness	Improvement Check Date
1.	a. b. c. d.	1. 2. 3.	
2.	a. b. c. d.	1. 2. 3.	
3.	a. b. c. d.	1. 2. 3.	
4.	a. b. c. d.	1. 2. 3.	

Are You Time Conscious?

Unless you cultivate respect for time and are continually conscious of its passage, you are apt to waste it. This quiz should tell you how much "time sensitivity" you have.

1. Do you know how much one hour of your time is worth?

2. Is your day's schedule of activities firmly in your mind when you arrive at your office?

3. Do you have a fairly accurate idea of what you ought to get done this week? This month? This quarter?

4. Have you delegated as much work as possible to subordinates?

5. Do you weigh the time requirements of various tasks before assigning them to others or undertaking them yourself?

6. Do you wade right into high-priority, tough and unpleasant jobs rather than devoting too much time to things you like to do?

7. Do you carry a notebook with you for jotting down ideas, information, insights, etc., rather than relying on your memory?

8. Do you use modern technology to save time — e.g., calculators, dictating machines, conference telephone calls, etc.?

9. Do you know how to screen visitors and phone calls?

10. Is there a steady flow of clear communication between you and your people?

11. Do you consciously appraise — and police — your use of leisure time?

12. Have you developed routine ways of handling routine matters?

13. When things are going well, do you take advantage of the momentum by tackling other tough chores — or do you ease off?

14. Do you challenge the way things are done — because you think there is always a more efficient way to get things done?

15. Do you have some "fill-in" jobs in case you suddenly find some spare time (e.g., a broken appointment)?

Three or more "no's" suggest it's time to change your ways!

Worksheet:
What's Your Time Worth?

Before going on, let's see what you think are your most
serious time problems. First, rank each of the possibilities on
the left side of the chart below in terms of severity.

Not a Problem for Me	Neutral	Serious Problem for Me	Problem	First Step I Should Take
			Doing everything myself	
			Worrying about problems	
			Participating in endless meetings	
			Handwriting reports or letters	
			Procrastinating	
			Engaging in long-winded conversations	
			Coping with recurring emergencies	

When you have ranked each item, go back and enter in the
column on the right the first step you should take to deal with
that time-wasting activity.

Don't be discouraged if you are guilty of several of these time-
wasting habits. We all are guilty at one time or another. No one
ever has "enough" time. Yet, everyone has all the time there is —
24 hours each day. This is the great paradox of time. It is the one
resource that is distributed equally to all of us.

To help get a handle on your time, start with these basics:

Keys to Managing Time

1. Time Analysis

A daily log of activities for at least one week, taken in fifteen-minute increments, is essential as a basis for effective time analysis. It should be repeated at least quarterly to avoid reverting to poor time management practices.

2. Anticipation

Anticipatory action is generally more effective than remedial action. "A stitch in time saves nine," so expect the unexpected and plan for it. Assume if anything can go wrong, it will. (Murphy's 3rd Law)

3. Planning

Every hour spent in effective planning saves three to four in execution and gets better results. Both long-range and daily planning, formulated after business hours the previous day or early the same day, in harmony with short-term objectives and events, are essential to effective utilization of personal time.

4. Flexibility

Flexibility in degree of scheduling personal time may be necessary to accommodate to forces beyond one's control. Time should not be over- or underscheduled.

5. Objectives and Priorities

More effective results are generally achieved through purposeful pursuit of planned objectives than by chance. Time available should be allocated to tasks in ordered sequence of priority. Set priorities and stick to them! Managers sometimes tend to spend time in amounts inversely related to the importance of tasks.

6. Deadlines

Imposing deadlines and exercising self-discipline in adhering to them aid managers in overcoming indecision, vacillation and procrastination.

7. Alternatives

In any given situation, failure to generate alternative solutions limits the likelihood of selecting the most effective course of action.

8. Consolidation

Similar tasks should be grouped within divisions of the work day to minimize interruptions (in taking and returning phone calls, for example), to economize in the utilization of resources and in personal expenditure of effort.

9. Pareto Principle/Concentration

A critical few efforts (around 20%) generally produce the great bulk of results (around 80%). This principle, also called "the 20/80 Law" has led effective managers to concentrate their efforts on the "critical few" events. This increases the likelihood of such events happening and, therefore, of achieving maximum results.

10. Effectiveness

Efficiency may be defined as doing any job right ... effectiveness as doing the right job right. Effort, however efficient, will tend to be ineffective if performed on the wrong tasks, at the wrong time or with unintended consequences.

11. Delegation/Decision Level

Authority for decision-making should be delegated to the lowest level possible, consistent with good judgment and available facts.

12. Upward Delegation

Managers tend to encourage upward (reverse) delegation unwittingly by encouraging dependence of subordinates upon them for answers. This results in their doing the work of their subordinates.

13. Minimizing Routine and Avoiding Detail

Routine tasks of low value to overall objectives should be minimized, consolidated, delegated or eliminated to the extent possible. Managers should divorce themselves from unnecessary detail and selectively neglect all but essential information. This has been termed "the need not to know."

"When I first started working I used to dream of the day when I might be earning the salary I'm starving on now."

14. Limited Response and Selective Neglect

Response to problems and demands upon time should be limited to the real needs of the situation. Some problems left alone go away. By selectively ignoring these problems that tend to resolve themselves, much time and effort can be conserved for more useful pursuits. (The Principle of Calculated Neglect.)

15. Exception Management

Only significant deviations of actual from planned performance should be reported to the responsible executive to conserve his time and abilities.

16. Visibility

Keeping visible those things you intend doing increases the certainty of achieving your objectives. You can't do what you can't remember. Rely on a filing system or checklists.

17. Brevity

Promoting clarity and understanding.

18. Tyranny of the Urgent

Managers live in constant tension between the urgent and the important. The urgent task demands instant action and drives out the important from our consciousness. Managers, thus, are tyrannized by the urgent and respond unwittingly to the endless pressures of the moment. In so doing, they neglect the long-term consequences of more important tasks left undone.

19. Crisis Management

Managers often manage-by-crisis, that is, they treat every problem as if it were a crisis. This over-response syndrome causes anxiety, impaired judgment, hasty decisions, wasted time and effort.

20. Interruption Control

Arrangement of and controls over activities should be designed to minimize the number, impact and duration of interruptions. Be tactful, but forthright.

Keys to Managing Time

Effective use of time has 2 major results:

1. We get more done, and

2. We feel better about our progress.

Our outlook and the world become less complicated. We look forward to going to work. Co-workers and bosses begin to notice.

Poor Use of Time Means...

1. **Excessive Tension**. If you are constantly beset by tension, you will tire quickly, both physically and mentally, and fail to function effectively.

2. **Reliance on Excuses**. You can't retrieve the past. Excuses or explaining failures accomplishes nothing and wastes energy and time.

3. **Indecisiveness**. Shifting from one task to another and procrastinating on things that should be started right away.

4. **Perfectionism**. If you get too involved in doing things perfectly, you may never finish them.

5. **Negative Emotions**. Hostility, frustration and worry can sap your strength and keep you from accomplishing as much as you otherwise could. Procrastinators carry the burden for their undone work.

6. **Insecurity**. If you are unsure of your own abilities, you will waste time building up your ego and trying to impress others.

7. **Workaholism**. Working every minute, at home, on vacation, indicates a breakdown in use of time-management principles.

Are you guilty of any of the following? To find out, rate yourself on each point on the following page.

Beware: Top 15 Time-Wasters

My Self-Rating

Poor   Average   Excellent

1   2   3   4   5

Five time-wasters nearly always rank at or near the top of managers' lists:

1. Telephone Interruptions   __ __ __ __ __
2. Drop-in Visitors   __ __ __ __ __
3. Meetings (both scheduled & unscheduled) __ __ __ __ __
4. Crises   __ __ __ __ __
5. Lack of Objectives, Priorities & Deadlines __ __ __ __ __

Action to be taken:

These are closely followed by another group of five time thieves:

6. Cluttered Desk and Personal
   Disorganization   __ __ __ __ __
7. Ineffective Delegation and
   Involvement in Routine Detail   __ __ __ __ __
8. Attempting Too Much at Once
   and Unrealistic Time Estimates   __ __ __ __ __
9. Confused Responsibility & Authority __ __ __ __ __
10. Inadequate, Inaccurate and
    Delayed Information   __ __ __ __ __

Action to be taken:

Depending upon the managers, particular leadership styles and organization characteristics, other time-wasters often include:

11. Indecision and Procrastination   __ __ __ __ __
12. Lack of or Unclear Communication
    and Instruction   __ __ __ __ __
13. Inability to Say "No"   __ __ __ __ __
14. Lack of Controls, Standards and
    Progress Reports   __ __ __ __ __
15. Fatigue and Lack of Self-Discipline __ __ __ __ __

Action to be taken:

Now go back over your ratings and circle the lowest in each group of five. Write the action you will take below each group of time-wasters.

Let's take a look at how one manager spends one day at his office. After reading this example, you will be asked several questions. Keep in mind your typical day, and see if you notice any similarities.

Where Does the Time Go?

The alarm clock rang at precisely seven-twenty, and Tod Williams got up and out of bed. Exactly one hour and thirty-three minutes later, he walked into his vice-presidential offices at General Industrial Corporation, where he has spent most of his working life.

As he was driving to work, Tod had his car radio turned to the news station. There had been an interesting piece about a newly proposed Federal regulation that could seriously affect his company's ability to compete, were it to become a law. So Tod's first move after he sat down behind his large mahogany desk, piled high with papers, was to leaf through the morning newspaper in search of more details on the story.

On page seven, a story about a young runaway caught his eye. His own daughter just turned fourteen, and he was beginning to sense some of the troubles that might lie ahead for him and his wife. He read the story with interest. Then another story on the local school board consumed his attention for a while. Finally, he discovered the item he was looking for and read it straight through.

Putting aside the newspaper, he looked at his watch. "Nine-thirty," he said to himself. "I'm running late already. I'll have to settle down today and get through some of this paperwork that's been piling up."

Tod William's Work in Progress

Working with determination and steady concentration, Tod began sorting through the papers in the pile nearest him – his "important work" pile – looking for something he could begin with today. He found a report to read, leaned back and began going over the detailed technical specifications, page by page.

Afterwards, he wrote a brief memo to his engineering chief regarding the proposed modifications in the company's new line of calculators that the report seemed to call for. "It's best to discover the need for these changes and make them while the product is still under development," he wrote in his steady handwriting at one point. "I propose additional market research and product development efforts before we make any firm commitment to production."

C
A
S
E

S
T
U
D
Y

Tod put the memo in his "out" box and, stuffing the report on an overcrowded shelf behind his desk, turned back to his "important work" pile. He began shuffling through, looking again for an item that was ripe. He glanced quickly over his desk. There were five distinct piles of paper on it. The one nearest him, on his right, was the "important work" pile. It was about six inches high. Beyond that and toward the front of the big desk was another taller pile of "important work, but not really important." Here Tod kept items that he would like to work on as soon as he got more time.

On the left side of the desk Tod piled routine reports and other technical reading he had to find time for. Next to this were files of relatively routine work already in progress. Tod rarely needed to turn to this pile unless something from his "in" box sent him there or unless a subordinate or someone outside the company inadvertently reminded him of one of the projects in that pile. In a third pile, he kept newspaper clippings, magazine articles, brief notes and other bits and pieces of ideas and facts retained for use later on. They were piled in no particular order on the left front corner of his desk, and from time to time Tod would leaf through the pile searching for some tidbit of information he seemed to recall having placed there a while ago. It was always an interesting search, even if he didn't always find what he was looking for.

Back at his "important work" pile, Tod came across a memo reminding him that he had delegated a particular assignment to one of his most promising subordinates a few weeks ago. Since then, he'd been so busy he hadn't had time to follow up on the delegated assignment. So now Tod decided to call in the subordinate to discuss his progress to date.

While waiting, Tod sorted briefly through his incoming mail, placing each item into its appropriate pile and throwing out the junk mail that usually made up a good part of his daily "in" box contents.

Questions

1. On a scale of one to ten, evaluate Tod's time-management ability on the basis of what you know about him so far. Defend your judgment with reasons and specific references to the case.

2. What do you feel should be Tod's highest priority for improvement in time management? How would you introduce him to your understanding of the difficulties he is experiencing?

3. What recommendations would you make, as a means of improving Tod's ability to manage his time?

4. Does Tod work well under pressure? Do you?

5. In what ways do you need to organize your work better?

6. Do you put first things first?

_____sometimes _____often _____usually

7. What two jobs should you do tomorrow?

8. What two jobs could you delegate to lighten your work load?

Up to this point, we have discussed some basic do's and don'ts of time management. You should now be able and ready to take a close look at one of your typical days. In the next several pages, you will complete and compare a Daily Time Log. Follow the instructions carefully.

Daily Time Log

A. List date and goals for the day — in terms of results, not activities (e.g., complete agenda within time allocated for sales meetings — not hold sales meeting.).

B. Record all significant acts in terms of results during each 15-minute period. DO NOT wait until noon or the end of the day, or the major benefit will be lost.

C. Answer the questions on page 54 immediately following Daily Time Log completion.

Daily Time Log

Date_____

Goals: 1._____

2._____

3._____

TIME	ACTION	PRIORITY	COMMENT/DISPOSITION/RESULTS
		1= Important & Urgent 2= Important Not Urgent 3= Urgent Not Imp. 4= Routine	Delegate to_____ Train _____to handle Next time ask for recommendation Next time say "No" Consolidate/Eliminate/Cut Time Other
8:00			
8:15			
8:30			
8:45			
9:00			
9:15			
9:30			
9:45			
10:00			
10:15			
10:30			
10:45			
11:00			
11:15			
11:30			
11:45			
12:00			
12:15			
12:30			
12:45			

Daily Time Log

TIME	ACTION	PRIORITY	COMMENT/DISPOSITION/RESULTS
		1= Important & Urgent 2= Important Not Urgent 3= Urgent Not Imp. 4= Routine	Delegate to_____ Train _____to handle Next time ask for recommendation Next time say "No" Consolidate/Eliminate/Cut Time Other
1:00			
1:15			
1:30			
1:45			
2:00			
2:15			
2:30			
2:45			
3:00			
3:15			
3:30			
3:45			
4:00			
4:15			
4:30			
4:45			
5:00			
5:15			
5:30			
Eve.			

Time Log Review Questions

1. Did setting daily goals and times for completion improve my effectiveness? Why? Why not?

2. What was the longest period of time without interruption?

3. In order of importance, which interruptions were most costly?

4. What can be done to eliminate or control them?
   a. Which telephone calls were unnecessary?
   b. Which telephone calls could have been shorter or more effective?
   c. Which visits were unnecessary?
   d. Which visits could have been shorter or more effective?

5. How much time was spent in meetings?
   a. How much was necessary?
   b. How could more have been accomplished in less time?

6. Did you tend to record "activities" or "results"?

7. How many of your daily goals contributed directly to your long-range goals and objectives?

8. Did a "self-correcting" tendency appear as you recorded your actions?

9. What two or three steps could you now take to improve your effectiveness?

You have a plain bar of iron worth about $5.

Made into a horseshoe, it's worth about $11.

Made into screwdrivers, it's worth about $15.

Made into needles, it's worth about $3,500.

The same is true of another kind of material: you. Your value is determined by what you decide to make of yourself.

Take time to analyze your "Time Log" using the Keys to
Managing Time on pp. 44-46. Note problems, in terms of
severity, and list possible solutions – what should be done.

Analysis of Your Time Management

PROBLEM	PRIORITY (Rank)	RECOMMENDATION (What Should Be Done)

How does your analysis help you with your time
management?

Time Flies and Fills

An incident at a state mental hospital in California has definite implications for the way we manage our time.

A newly degreed intern was asked to observe patient behavior at noon in the exercise yard. On his first day, he noticed a patient pulling a wheelbarrow around the yard — upside down. After several days of seeing the same routine, the doctor asked the patient why he was doing this.

"Well, Doc," the patient explained, "I used to come out here every day as you have seen me, at noontime, and push my wheelbarrow right side up around the yard. And do you know what happened to my wheelbarrow by the end of the hour? People dumped so much garbage into it that I couldn't push it. So all I do now is turn it upside down and no one dumps into my wheelbarrow anymore."

Moral:

Nature abhors a vacuum. When there is a state of emptiness, something quickly moves to fill the void. Similarly, we might view the nature of time by the "law of time displacement," which states simply, but irrevocably, that "every moment of time you have will be displaced by someone or something."

One way to keep from "filling" time indiscriminately is to:

Intercept Those Interruptions

Try these solutions to "reclaim" some of that valuable time.

Problems	Solutions
1. Ego — makes you feel important to be asked advice or have drop-ins	Recognize. Be available at lunch.
2. Desire to be kept informed, to stay on the grapevine.	Accomplish this on a planned and more certain basis.
3. Fear of offending.	Don't be over-sensitive. Take time log and carefully assess number and impact of all interruptions.
4. Ineffective screening techniques.	Train secretary to screen visitors and calls without offending.
5. Ineffective monitoring of visits. (Scheduled & Unscheduled)	Have secretary interrupt (by phone or in person) to remind boss (and visitor if desired) of approaching end of time available. Wrist alarm is self-reminder. Preset time limit on visitors; foreshadow end of visit. Log time scheduled for appointments, time actually spent, and reason for discrepancy (if any).
6. Making decisions below your level.	Make only the decisions subordinates can't.
7. Requiring subordinates to "check with you" excessively.	Manage by exception.
8. Failure to delegate.	Do nothing you can delegate. Problems on matters delegated should be taken to persons handling the matters.
9. Desire to socialize.	Do elsewhere.
10. No plans for unavailability.	Quiet hour; modified "Open Door" policy.
11. Encouraging staff to bring their problems to you.	This encourages dependence and dropping in with questions. Encourage initiative, risk-taking and decision-making.

Visitors — Unscheduled and Scheduled

	Problems	**Solutions**
Telephone	1. No secretary.	Have switchboard screen calls. Use cut-off switch.
	2. To appear available.	Call-backs.
	3. No plan.	Reserve time to plan.
	4. Enjoy socializing.	Elsewhere.
	5. Lack self-discipline.	Learn to group calls.
	6. To remain informed and involved.	Accomplish in planned and more certain way.
	7. Poor screening.	Train secretary to intercept — divert.
	8. Ego.	Recognize. Control.
	9. Misdirected calls.	Train.
	10. Lack of coordination.	Delegate.
	11. Unable to terminate.	Be brief. Use egg timer. Hang up on yourself mid-sentence. Say "thanks for calling" or "I'm sorry, I have another call."
	12. Uncertain of responsibilities.	Clarify.
	13. Fear of offending.	Don't be over-sensitive.

	Problems	**Solutions**
Meetings	1. Lack of purpose.	No meeting without a purpose in writing, if possible.
	2. Lack of agenda.	No meeting without an agenda.
	3. Wrong people/too many.	Only those needed present.
	4. Wrong time.	Ensure opportune timing.
	5. Wrong place.	Select location consistent with objectives of meeting: freedom from interruptions, physical equipment necessary, minimum of travel for majority of people.

6. No planning.

Allow for and schedule appropriate planning time.

7. Too many meetings.

Test need for "regular" meetings. Occasionally don't hold — see what happens...or cut time allowed in half — for those tending to last a long time.

8. Inadequate motive.

Provide written notice with all essentials, including expected contribution and materials necessary for preparation.

9. Not starting on time.

Start on time. (By delaying for late arrivals, the leader penalizes those arriving on time and rewards those who come late!)

10. Socializing.

Reserve socializing for better places. Get down to business.

11. Allowing interruptions.

Set policy and let everyone know. Wherever possible, allow no interruptions except for clear-cut emergencies. Take messages for delivery at coffee break and lunch time.

12. Wandering from agenda.

Expect and demand adherence to agenda. Resist "hidden agenda" ploys.

13. Failure to set ending time or time allotment for each subject.

Time limit the meeting and each item on the agenda to place discussion time in accordance with importance of subject.

14. Failure to end on time.

Do end on time. Otherwise no one plans for the time immediately following.

15. Indecision.

Keep objective in mind and move toward it.

III. Meetings (continued)

Problems	Solutions
16. Deciding without adequate information.	Ensure requisite information will be available before convening meetings.
17. Failure to summarize conclusions and to record in minutes.	Summarize conclusions to ensure agreement and remind participants of assignments. Record decisions, assignments and deadlines in concise minutes. Distribute within one day.
18. Failure to follow up.	Ensure effective follow-up on all decisions. List uncompleted items under "Unfinished Business" at beginning of next agenda. Request status report until complete.
19. Failure to terminate committees when business or objectives accomplished.	Take committee inventory. Abolish those whose mission has been accomplished.

The "Natural Breaks"

By using these exercises and logs, you can salvage more time for important things. By working around "natural breaks" you may also be able to accomplish major projects.

As you look at the calendar, there are natural breaks in your work schedule. They may be vacation times, three-day weekends, holidays, a birthday or other special day. Select three or four of these "break" times in the next three months. Then plan your future schedule to take the greatest possible advantage of these breaking points. For each chosen date, set the goal of completing some appropriate assignment or activity. Plan to start something new and challenging on the other side of each break.

Keep the time schedule for the next three months and work to accomplish your goals and to get your new projects started — all on schedule. Use the worksheet on the next page. You may want to make a photocopy for each day or possibly one copy for each week.

"It isn't what you know that counts, it's what you think of in time."

Project or Assignment to Be Completed	Chosen Calendar/Break Dates	New Project or Assignment to Be Started

As you look at each day's schedule, you will see that there are natural breaks there too. If there is a short time between two scheduled blocks of time, what tasks would be appropriate to use the time to greatest benefit?

Which things can be handled when you are waiting for an appointment?

Which tasks could be handled during travel time?

Consider these transitional times carefully. Some tasks can be adapted to make use of time that would otherwise be lost.

In 1983 James Garner was awarded a Purple Heart for having been wounded in Korea 32 years before.

"I got it in the backside," recalled Garner, "I went into a foxhole head first, and I was a little late."

Getting Work Done

Many managers and supervisors have specific methods for getting work done. All of these approaches have merit and, under certain circumstances, all may be used. Try a different task to fit the need. Listed below are several to choose from.

1. **Do it immediately!** Rush jobs deserve priority, but remember to weigh the jobs for importance.

2. **Handle tough or unpleasant tasks first.** The problem of avoiding an unpleasant task is that you carry its emotional burden with you, and it slows you down.

3. **Take care of the easier problems first.** Since doing the unpleasant task first has been widely encouraged, it may seem unwise to do the easy thing first. Yet, this method does have its uses — for example, at a meeting where controversial decisions must be reached. Better relations are likely to result if the less problematic items are settled first. Also, sometimes you can handle many small tasks quickly and have them out of the way.

4. **Do the jobs in the order of their importance.** This is generally good unless the important tasks are all very tiring or boring. It is possible that this approach may tempt you to neglect or put off certain tasks. Use this strategy only as long as lower priority items will be done within a reasonable time.

5. **Alternate difficult and easy tasks.** Alternating will give you a rest and something to look forward to. This variety can increase your motivation.

6. **Group similar tasks.** It makes sense to complete several jobs using the same or related supplies in other ways before going on to the next item. It reduces duplication of effort and gives you a warm-up. Watch that you don't use this approach to avoid unappealing tasks.

7. **Change tasks about every two hours.** This approach is especially helpful in doing routine, monotonous tasks, for a different type of job can relieve boredom, lift spirits and give you something to anticipate.

Now that you have new tools for managing your time and getting work done, it's necessary to...

Plan Your Progress

Complete the following statements. Mark your calendar so that in six months you look at this page and see how well you have managed time.

I.   **My top long-term career goals are:**

1. _____
2. _____
3. _____

II. **The most important of these is:**

III. **Three tasks that will most help me attain this most important long-term goal are:**

1. _____
2. _____
3. _____

IV. **The first task I must complete to achieve it is:**

V.   **The three most crucial steps for the next six months are:**

1. _____
2. _____
3. _____

VI. **The single most important step for the next six months is:**

VII. **Three tasks that will help me complete this most important step for the next six months are:**

1. _____
2. _____
3. _____

VIII. **The first task I must complete to reach it is:**

Remember: No one else can do this for you. Your continued career growth and development is in your hands. You must plan and monitor it yourself!

Time management can make you more productive at work. It can also greatly improve your personal life by providing opportunities to do those things you most enjoy.

Summary: Do's and Don'ts

Don't —

- Solve problems that aren't vital to your primary objectives (posterities).

- Work on problems that have no current solution.

- Spend time solving smaller problems that subordinates could handle.

But Be Sure To —

- Work on the big, important jobs and leave the smaller less important jobs until later.

- Work on projects that are most likely to succeed rather than on those that are sure to fail.

- Invest time and effort on areas where growth is both needed and possible.

Questions for Personal Development

1. What is the major emphasis of this chapter?

2. What do you feel is the most important thing you learned from this chapter?
   1)
   2)
   3)

3. How can you apply what you learned to your current job?
   1)
   2)
   3)

4. What objectives will you set to improve? By when (date)?
   1)
   2)
   3)

5. Who can help you most in applying what you learned in this chapter?

6. What are the major roadblocks you expect that may hinder your progress in applying what you learned in this chapter?

   Roadblock   **Why?**
   1)
   2)
   3)

7. How will you communicate the most important points in this chapter to your key people?

8. What preparation is necessary for this introduction?

9. What changes do you expect to make that will achieve greater motivation of your team?

   Change   **By when – date?**

   1)

   2)

   3)

10. How will you monitor to assure that performance has improved, i.e., productivity has increased? (Reports, meetings, etc.)

11. What work-related problems concern you most in evaluating how you will benefit from this chapter?

12. Once you've accomplished several milestones, how will you continue developing new ideas and objectives related to this chapter?

13. How would you summarize the change you expect to see in yourself one year from now as a result of what you learned in this chapter?

*C*HAPTER 3

Planning

Unless an organization is continuously planning for the future, it will be difficult to accomplish any type of objective. Where does planning begin? It begins with a clear statement of purpose or mission. Your mission statement should be a broad, general statement that commits to specific purposes and includes any restrictions. As goals and objectives are developed, the meaning of the statement will be made explicit. These statements should always be put in writing and distributed to everyone who has a stake in the organization.

Between the statement or development of objectives and their fulfillment are a variety of environmental influences affecting your operation. Although often intangible, they are nonetheless very real. Successful managers are able to evaluate these conditions and determine what will and will not work in their organizations. This is known as "gauging the environment." As you plan you will be more successful if you develop this knack.

Managers who have this ability to gauge the environment know what they can sell to their people and what they cannot. These managers also learn to understand and adjust to certain facts. For example, they learn to cope with the fact that some units will be slower in implementing new programs than others; that certain communications will break down or misfire; that some units can never seem to get off dead center without being prodded.

The "bridge" between planning and results is objectives. But top management alone can't achieve objectives. Whether you work in one department or manage several departments, it will be worth your while to consider:

Why Organizations Lose Their Effectiveness

It is natural that each department in an organization should attempt to create order to gain efficiency. The routines become firmly set and little slows down their development. Each individual department builds higher and higher barriers to keep outsiders from disturbing its routines.

What can be done? There are no easy answers. However, rigid and excessive routines can be prevented by introducing constructive change.

This involves:

1. Recognizing the dangers of rigidity.

2. Giving managers credit in performance reviews for working effectively with other departments.

3. Using a mediator to work out serious departmental squabbles.

4. Transferring people occasionally from one department to another so they can get an overview and understand the workings of other departments.

The ten questions on the next page are designed to help you develop your planning skills.

> *"No business opportunity is ever lost. If you fumble it, your competitor will find it."*

Develop Your Planning Skills

Score each question on the following scale in the blank provided.

Definite Strength	**Moderately Effective**	**Average Performance**	**Rarely Effective**	**Definite Weakness**
10 – 9	8 – 7	6 – 5	4 – 2	1 – 0

1. Do I have a plan for spotting problems in the regular workflow and starting remedial action?

   _____   _____   _____   _____   _____

2. Have I set up checkpoints for monitoring work in progress?

   _____   _____   _____   _____   _____

3. Am I prepared to give answers regarding the work being done in my unit?

   _____   _____   _____   _____   _____

4. Do I have a grasp of possible problems involved in making changes in procedures or routines?

   _____   _____   _____   _____   _____

5. Do I work out — and stick to—deadlines?

   _____   _____   _____   _____   _____

6. Do I block out schedules, coordinating shared work responsibilities?

   _____   _____   _____   _____   _____

7. Do monthly reports for my unit indicate excessive overtime, failure to meet schedules or serious complaints?

   _____   _____   _____   _____   _____

8. Does my unit have recent unexplainable crises?

   _____   _____   _____   _____   _____

9. Have I trained subordinates so that work would continue even if I were absent or promoted?

   _____   _____   _____   _____   _____

10. Can I evaluate accurately the potential and limitations of people I supervise?

   _____   _____   _____   _____   _____

SUB TOTALS   _____   _____   _____   _____   _____

TOTAL SCORE _____

What areas need some of your attention for development? See Scoring Key at the end of this chapter, page 82.

> *"I've never known a person who was lucky for a long time. They all deserved what they had. There is no such thing as a lucky marathon runner."*

In the next case study, Bob Abbott has some real problems with planning. After reading it, rate Bob's skill as a planner using the ten questions on page 71.

"What's Going Wrong?"

Bob Abbott, age 35, and generally thought of as the best programmer at World Wide, Inc., was offered the job as team leader. He accepted it after considerable uncertainty. He really liked his work as a programmer, but the new job was a promotion, a real compliment to him and paid a great deal more than his position as programmer. Bob's predecessor was moving to a higher position as a project manager. His predecessor had a reputation as a good manager and cautioned Bob about the necessity of spending his time planning and delegating rather than doing the work himself. They discussed the tendency for those in their first managerial position to become too personally involved in the work, particularly when they are well qualified technically.

Bob was determined to be a good manager. He insisted on a high quality level, especially for reports that would go outside his team. His staff included nine full-time people. After a short while, problems began to appear. Bob found himself out there "pitching in" when there was a problem. The paper on Bob's desk was mounting — specifications to be done, new programs to be evaluated, etc. Bob was pleased with his relationships with his employees, but the team was constantly in a series of "crises." A fair amount of Bob's time seemed to be taken up with employees running into his office to check their work progress. Yet, they were highly motivated people with a good record for competence. Bob had to conclude that he was doing something wrong. He decided to visit his former boss to ask for suggestions.

Review Questions

You are Bob's former boss. What do you see that might be causing the problems? (Write your answer below.)

What would you suggest that Bob do to change things? (Write your answer below.)

Bob's environment definitely needs to be "primed" for planning. Following the steps below would have been helpful to him ...and might be to you as well. These planning steps make up a ...

Planning Primer

1. Define Goals

Brief — in writing — specific — measurable.

2. Collect All Relevant Data

Best methods — changed circumstances or conditions.

3. Select the Best Method

Eliminate unnecessary steps — simplify — determine priorities.

4. Develop the Plan

Select and train people — provide resources — eliminate obstacles.

5. Implement the Plan

Revise as necessary.

6. Follow Up

Be persistent.

As you begin the planning process, you have crossed the first hurdle. You have gone past the resistance stage. Be aware, however, that the reasons for resistance can resurface at any

> *"Winners expect to win. Life is a self-fulfilling prophecy."*

time. Review this list whenever you feel you are becoming "side-tracked." For now, check which of the factors are applicable to you personally and to your work unit at the present time.

Why Planning Is Resisted

	Applicable to Me Now		
A. Because Personally I Am:	Yes	No	Unsure
—Not excited by the predictable	____	____	____
—Anxious to be in control	____	____	____
—Limited in self-confidence	____	____	____
—Inclined to overlook shortcomings	____	____	____
—Undecided about personal goals	____	____	____
—Hesitant to change	____	____	____

	Applicable to My Unit Now		
B. Because Organizationally We Are:	Yes	No	Unsure
—Preoccupied with present problems	____	____	____
—Intrigued by the unknown, yet afraid of the uncertain	____	____	____
—Fearful about failure	____	____	____
—Lacking in information	____	____	____
—Pressed for time	____	____	____
—Apprehensive about decisions that may be wrong	____	____	____

Which of your personal answers in Section A above do you think will have the greatest impact on your career? Why?

Which of your organizational answers in Section B above do you think are most serious for your employer? Why?

"As he was going about the task of selecting people for his new computer company, H. Ross Perot posted signs to remind his employees that eagles don't flock — you have to find them one at a time."

To get yourself focused during the early planning stages, answer the following questions. Take time to think each one through carefully. Your ultimate plan will be as good as your preparation.

Questions for Planners

— What can I personally do to make the greatest impact on the organization?

— What new and smarter ways can I find to do the job? What are my subordinates' ideas? Have I explored the full range of possibilities before discarding any idea?

— What roadblocks need to be eliminated to allow me to make the greatest possible contribution to the organization?

— Have I determined how much time is involved in completing my proposal(s)?

Now, thinking in terms of team performance, answer these questions:

— What direction do I need to give my team to ensure that its activities contribute directly to area performance?

— What am I or my team doing that has nothing to do with my objectives or that may be working against achieving them?

— What am I doing that is duplicated elsewhere?

Your answers to these questions should give you a much clearer sense of direction for planning.

> *"Those who are easily defeated have hundreds of reasons why things won't work when all they need is one reason why they will!"*

The challenge at this point is to turn your plans into results. Here are some specific suggestions. To determine how each point may be applicable in your present situation, make a note in the left margin regarding where it applies and with whom.

From Paper Plans to Action

Interpret Your Plan As You Go

There is a need to interpret plans in accord with their purpose. Sometimes this requires modification, but with care. Plans are subject to change. Part of nearly every plan has to be re-edited in the light of events as action proceeds.

Divide and Conquer

Two hints may be useful in overcoming the common fault of procrastination. The first is: Commit yourself. Having promised performance by a set date, you find yourself honor bound to fulfill it. The second is: Do not tackle an accumulation of work like a bulldozer. Break the pile down into small, accessible units, and grapple with them one by one.

Schedule Subjobs

When a plan reaches the action stage, it is necessary to assign proportions and priorities as much as possible. The major schedule will be set in the master planning (completion by such-and-such a date). The detailed scheduling remains so that all parts fit into the ultimate result.

Functions

Distribute the functions involved in the jobs according to time. Dating back from the target completion date, what must be done today, tomorrow? Sequence is vital. If the nature of the job does not dictate in what order operations are to be done, perform the essential things first.

Simplify Layout

The best role for the supervisor is to put useful tools where they can easily and quickly be found. Streamline your work with as few hindrances to its flow as possible.

Where does this apply?	With whom does this apply?

76

Integrate Effort

Brief everyone who is concerned with the project as much as necessary to assure integration of effort. Share your work. Delegate to others, those who will do the work and co-operate with people in other departments.

Act With Precision

It is a good practice to deliberate with caution, but to act with decision and promptness. Consider paperwork: It is a good rule to dispose of a piece of paper when you first pick it up.

Seek Better Ways

Anticipation is just as important as the capability to handle crises. When you have had a job in process for a reasonable length of time, take a look at it to learn if there is an easier or more efficient way of doing it. Group the activities so that one follows the other with the least disruption and effort. An even pace, rather than a series of spurts, makes the best use of your energy so that you effect the most with the least effort.

Get On With It!

You cannot begin a task effectively by coasting. Start with energy. Initial inertia is a law of all life. **It takes more effort to get going than to keep going.** Fortune does not smile on those who, having prepared to do a job, hesitate. Dr. Donald A. Laird wrote in his book, *The Technique of Getting Things Done,* "Don't look at a thing: Start it. Don't put off a day: Start it. Don't pretend you must think it over: Start it. Don't start halfheartedly: Put everything you can muster into your start."

The Professional Touch

Men and women with these abilities are in great demand. They have the quality of concentrating upon goals attainable in the given situation and solving immediate problems as they arise.

Where does this apply?	With whom does this apply?

Summary:
Testing Ideas

- What is the ultimate contribution of this idea to unit performance if fully implemented?

  My Response:

- What are the chances this idea will be implemented if I really get behind it and push?

  My Response:

- Does the idea have application elsewhere?

  My Response:

- Does the idea conflict with another group's objectives?

  My Response:

- Will the idea help me meet my objectives?

  My Response:

- Are there impediments to implementing the idea? What are they?

  My Response:

- Can I eliminate the impediments myself, or do I need help?

  My Response:

- Who can authorize action on my idea — me, my supervisor, a manager?

  My Response:

- How can I sell my idea up the line?

  My Response:

- Do I have the resources to implement my idea without impairing other individual or group objectives?

  My Response:

- Can I do it by working harder?

  My Response:

- How can I get more resources if I need them?

  My Response:

As a result of this testing procedure, some ideas would be discarded, some would be readily accepted, others would require investigation and refinement. Once an idea is judged feasible, it should be put into an action plan to determine **who** will do **what** by **when.**

> *Remember —*
>
> *Effective leaders can't lose sleep over the possible adverse results of every action they take throughout the course of their plan. If they do, they'd be better off taking orders from someone else! So would their organizations!*

Questions for Personal Development

1. What is the major emphasis of this chapter?

2. What do you feel are the most important things you learned from this chapter?

   1)

   2)

   3)

3. How can you apply what you learned to your current job?

   1)

   2)

   3)

4. What objectives will you set to improve? By when (date)?

   1)

   2)

   3)

5. Who can help you most in applying what you learned in this chapter?

6. What are the major roadblocks you expect that may hinder your progress in applying what you learned in this chapter?

   Roadblock: **Why?**

   1)

   2)

   3)

7. How will you communicate the most important points in this chapter to your key people?

8. What preparation is necessary for this introduction?

9. What changes do you expect to make that will achieve greater motivation of your team?

Change   **By when (date)?**

1)

2)

3)

10. How will you monitor to assure that performance has improved, i.e., productivity has increased? (Reports, meetings, etc.)

11. What work-related problems concern you most in evaluating how you will benefit from this chapter?

12. Once you've accomplished several milestones, how will you continue developing new ideas and objectives related to this chapter?

13. How would you summarize the change you expect to see in yourself one year from now as a result of what you learned in this chapter?

**Scoring
Key**

How Did You Do?

Take your total from the Planning Skills test and compare it to the figures below:

If your score is:

80-100	Planning is a definite strength.
60-79	You are moderately effective as a planner.
40-59	Planning is a weakness. You probably have trouble meeting deadlines. Unless you take action, trouble may lie ahead.
39 or below	If you're not in trouble already, you've been fortunate. It's time to take action to improve your planning skills.

*C*HAPTER 4

Performance-Based Management — PBM

As the behavioral sciences have evolved in recent years, so has our knowledge of professional management. Managers now must get work done effectively with concern for people and their personal development. In striving to meet both these requirements, Performance-Based Management has emerged as the most systematic and effective approach — balancing satisfaction and productivity.

This section will clarify the goal-setting process and present specific methods, examples and exercises to assist you in developing skills in goal-setting and measuring progress.

Measurable goals in key result areas combined with action plans will pay off!

Key Management Areas to Be Monitored

In what areas do you find the majority of your problems as a manager? Rank each of these ten areas as A (serious problem for me), B (modest problem), or C (no problem).

My Ranking

A   B   C

___ ___ ___   1. Poor planning

___ ___ ___   2. Unmeasurable goals

___ ___ ___   3. Inadequate controls

___ ___ ___   4. Increasing costs

___ ___ ___   5. Ineffective training

___ ___ ___   6. Poor communication

___ ___ ___   7. Ineffective delegation

___ ___ ___   8. Low morale

___ ___ ___   9. Too much change

___ ___ ___   10. Too little change

We have worked on skills to cope with some of these problems. You may be saying, "There's room for more growth." Well, how do you measure up in the next section?

Management Inconsistencies

If we are going to see marked improvement, it is essential that we take an honest look at what we're doing. Unfortunately, what we say is often "at odds" with what actually happens.

We May Say	But in Reality
"I plan."	Objectives are vague and contradictory.
"I make fact-based decisions."	Emotions, opinions and personalities come first.
"I manage by objectives."	They may be my objectives, but the people who will do the work have not been involved.
"I believe in job enrichment."	Pay is considered the only motivator.
"I use control systems to measure."	Things measured are unimportant.
"I do my job."	Organizational politics and power plays consume much time.

> "Let us be thankful for the fools. But for them, the rest of us could not succeed."

Goals for an organization must be based on...

Preparing a Needs Analysis

Before setting goals for our work group, we must know what is in the best interest of the organization. To do that we must be as honest and open as we can be about determining the present situation.

Because goal-setting includes determining where a work group wants to be and how it is going to get there, it is necessary first of all to look at **where it is now.** Depending on where it is now, one plan of action may be more appropriate than another.

Within an organization, it is quite normal to have differences of opinion as to the current situation. Until some of these differences are reconciled, until we can agree on major assets and liabilities, until we have some consensus as to our basic purpose, we won't get very far trying to set goals that can be supported by everyone. We must start with a realistic evaluation of the present, a needs analysis.

Then we should start thinking about where we want to be a year from now. What results would be realistic in light of where we are starting from and where we would like to be?

When we move to consider goals for each unit within the organization, we will be seeking agreement among the key people at that level about its present and desired position.

We want to be sure we are honestly facing up to reality — that we are not overlooking or "glossing over" important factors. Different views should be discussed, not to determine who is "right" or "wrong" but to be as accurate as possible in identifying the most pressing needs before objectives are determined.

Here are the questions to be considered for a realistic analysis of the present situation prior to setting goals.

Where Are We Now?   ## Answers

A. What is our basic purpose?   Be brief; use key words only

B. What are our strengths?

C. What are our weaknesses?

D. Are we winning or
   losing in:

	Winning (examples)	Losing (examples)
1. Number served (volume)?	Sales up 10% this quarter	Profit down 5% on top 10 customers
2. Superiority of our service?	Order processing time cut by 2 hours	Still too high — losing customers
3. Quality of products?	Warrantee expenses down $300,000	Scrap material cost up $180,000
4. Customer satisfaction?	Customers retained up 15%	Average billing down 15%
5. Competitive position?	Gained 20% market share	Chief competitor gained 25% market share
6. Productivity of staff?	Engineer turnover down; clerical absenteeism down	Engineer turnover still over 35%
7. Training of replacements?	Two promotions into supervision in past year	No backups now for any management position

Goals and Action

Considering all factors in this Needs Analysis, we should set these goals to meet our highest priority needs. In other words, these are the areas where we must have goals to be certain that we are

1. maintaining our strengths, and
2. eliminating our weaknesses.

Now, use the form on the next page to complete a needs analysis of your work unit. Ideally it will be helpful to involve your co-workers and, best of all, your boss. Remember — be specific!

What are the questions to be considered for a realistic analysis of the present prior to setting goals?

Needs Analysis Questions

Where Are We Now?   Answers

A. What is our basic purpose? _____

B. What are our strengths? _____

C. What are our weaknesses? _____

D. Are we winning or losing in:

   1. Number or % of those
      served? _____

   2. Superiority of our service? _____

   3. Quality of products? _____

   4. Customer satisfaction? _____

   5. Competitive position? _____

   6. Productivity of staff? _____

   7. Training of replacements? _____

**Based on this analysis, what are the one-year goals of
your work group?**

Before deciding, consider:

   1. What weaknesses or "losses" do we want to correct?

   2. What strengths or "wins" do we want to maintain?

In reviewing your personal needs analysis, don't be surprised to find that inconsistencies exist. Is it possible to reconcile those inconsistencies? **Definitely!** Here are the steps that must be emphasized. By practicing them, you will be well on your way to eliminating your personal inconsistencies.

Reconciling Management Practice and Theory

1. State clear objectives.

2. Hold management accountable.

3. Align the interests of individuals with those of the organization.

4. Identify for each manager the path from effective performance to the rewards he or she values.

5. Reward people who perform.

6. Support creative decisions.

7. Set favorable examples.

Goals vs. Tasks

The following nine factors are basic managerial responsibilities. As you concentrate on them, consider whether you are goal-oriented or task-oriented. The difference is clear. This chapter will guide you toward becoming a goal-oriented individual. We will also discuss the process for establishing a goal-oriented environment.

Goal-Oriented Individual　　Task-Oriented Individual

	Self-Rating: Is this me?				Self-Rating: Is this me?	
	YES	NO			YES	NO
1. Seeks feedback and know-ledge of results. Wants evalua-tion of own performance. Wants concrete feedback.	___	___		1. Avoids feedback and evaluation. Seeks approval rather than performance evaluation.	___	___
2. Considers money a standard of achievement rather than an incentive to work harder.	___	___		2. Is directly influenced in job performance by money incentives. Work varies accordingly.	___	___
3. Seeks personal responsibility for work if goal achieve-ment is possible.	___	___		3. Avoids personal respon-sibility regardless of opportunities for success.	___	___
4. Performs best on jobs that can be improved. Prefers opportunities for creativity.	___	___		4. Prefers routine non-improvable jobs. Obtains no satisfaction from creativity.	___	___
5. Seeks goals with moderate risks.	___	___		5. Seeks goals with either very low or very high risks.	___	___
6. Obtains achievement satisfaction from solving difficult problems.	___	___		6. Obtains satisfaction not from problem-solving so much as from finishing a task.	___	___
7. Has high drive and physical energy directed toward goals.	___	___		7. May or may not have high drive. Energies are not goal-oriented.	___	___
8. Initiates action. Perceives suggestions as interference.	___	___		8. Follows others' directions. Receptive to suggestions.	___	___
9. Adjusts level of aspiration to realities of success and failure.	___	___		9. Maintains a constant level of aspiration regardless of success or failure.	___	___

1. Fill out this survey on your boss.

2. Fill out this survey for each employee.

Your response will tell you a great deal about your opportunity to create effective teamwork in your present position.

Have you recently thought about how goals are set in your area of responsibility? Does your boss set them for you or with you? Do you set them for or with your subordinates? This is important because the way a goal is set, or an assignment given, has a direct influence on reactions and results.

For example, some people think they must not only indicate what must be done, but must detail exactly how they want it done. They are not managing, because they are denying their people an opportunity to use their own thought, judgment and initiative. On the other hand, managers who negotiate desired results but, stop short of detailing how people should do their jobs, tend to keep their subordinates involved and interested. They allow them the satisfaction of working out solutions and thereby encourage creativity and innovation.

In effect, a participative or developmental style stimulates individuals to think. The pay-off can usually be noted in both better ideas and better morale.

> *"When we lose, I eat. When we win, I eat. I also eat when we're rained out."*
> Tommy Lasorda, Manager, Los Angeles Dodgers

A Helpful Planning Design

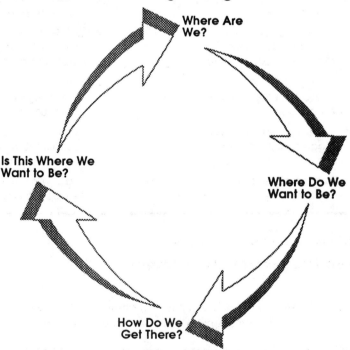

Where Are We?

Where Do We Want to Be?

How Do We Get There?

Is This Where We Want to Be?

Performance-Based Management (PBM) can lead us to our chosen destination.

PBM Definitions

PBM—Performance-Based Management is a continual process where managers periodically identify their common goals, define each individual's major areas of responsibility in terms of results expected and use these agreed-upon measures as guides for each operating department and for assessing individual contributions to the work of the entire organization. To understand PBM, you need to understand these definitions:

Objective — the results to be accomplished; what one will have to show for the expenditure of resources and energy. Objectives must be measurable and realistic, telling **what** will be changed, **how much, when** and **by whom.**

Goal — same as objective.

Mission or Purpose — a never-ending, ongoing reason for being. Something for which we constantly strive but will never completely achieve.

Key Result Area (KRA) — a key result area answers these questions: "What is it I am trying to measure?," "What am I accountable for?" and "What are the major components of my job?" KRAs are designated **before** measuring accomplishments.

Success Indicator — a way to measure change; tells us how to measure accomplishments; the yardsticks to be applied as time goes by to determine if we are heading in the right direction; a substitute phrase might be, "As measured by..."; the four broad types of indicators are quantity, quality, time and cost.

Activity — an expenditure of energy; a program; something one does as opposed to something one makes happen (creates); a means as opposed to an end.

Input — an asset; a resource or something needed to do work; a tool; a means as opposed to an end.

Output — what was accomplished; the outcome of productive effort; the value added by a wise selection among alternatives and the additional benefits enjoyed due to the timely and energetic expenditure of effort and resources.

Where Do We Want to Be?

How Do We Get There?

How Will We Know When We Get There?

Now that you've reviewed job-related and personal development goals, let's take a look at the total business process for an organization.

The PBM Cycle for Business Organizations

How Does PBM Work?

GATHER FACTS
(Internal)

- Sales
- Profits
- Products/Services
- Personnel
- Income
- Expense
- Organization

ORGANIZATION GOALS

- Sales by Product Line
- Net Profit by Prod. Line
- Research & Development
- Employee Productivity
- Customer Satisfaction
- Management Development
- Market Penetration
- Financial Requirements
- Operating Costs
- Community Relations
- Plant & Equipment
- Competitive Position

GATHER FACTS
(External)

- Markets
- Customers
- Competitors
- Community
- Government

ORGANIZATIONAL GOALS

SET UNIT OBJECTIVES

AGREE ON KEY RESULT AREAS—
SUCCESS INDICATORS
IMPROVEMENT PLANS

MAINTAIN PARTICIPATION
IMPLEMENT THE PLAN

EVALUATE RESULTS
APPRAISE MANAGERS
SET NEW OBJECTIVES

REVIEW PROGRESS
REMOVE OBSTACLES
REVISE IF NECESSARY

PBM — Guides to Action

1. Introduce from the top down.

2. Establish a definite installation schedule.

3. The greater the participation, the more favorable the effect upon results.

4. Start by setting clear goals for the PBM program itself. Follow with extensive training.

5. A results orientation in the organization (versus seniority, credentials, whom you know, who hired you, etc.).

6. Performance feedback at frequent intervals is necessary.

7. The best feedback is supportive and helpful, not judgmental.

8. Persist when key people object, falter or criticize the system.

9. Regular monitoring involves checks on attitude and relationships, as well as performance.

10. A dedication to accountability and measured progress in terms of who will do what by when.

> **Action – How to Make PBM Work for You**

Your Performance Profile

What are the key result areas of my job? What are the success indicators?

Key Result Examples:	**Success Indicator Examples:**
• Negotiate settlements	• Agreements reached before deadline
• Processing orders	• Time per order
• Machine maintenance	• Downtime
• Customer/client contact	• Retained or new customer/clients
• Selling	• Product/service sales volume/profit

On what basis do I judge my subordinates' performance?

On what basis does (should) my manager base my performance?

What is my responsibility in developing personnel?

If I were promoted, who would take my position? Is he or she ready now? If not, what is needed and how long would it take?

What type of training is needed to achieve the results I (we) must obtain?

What is my contribution to profits and control of expenses?

What changes are needed in my department in the next three months, six months, twelve months?

What things are needed for my own personal development in order for me to be successful?

> *"Great minds have purpose. Others have wishes."*
> Washington Irving

PBM — Activity vs. Results

There is an old saying that we begin by making habits, and end by habits making us. It is easy to let our lives and our work fall into a rut and our actions become mechanical and thoughtless. We become like processionary caterpillars.

Processionary caterpillars move through the trees in a long procession, one leading and the others following — each with his eyes half-closed and his head snugly fitted against the rear extremity of his predecessor.

Jean-Henri Fabre, the great French naturalist, after patiently experimenting with a group of these caterpillars, finally enticed them to the rim of a large flowerpot where he succeeded in getting the first one connected with the last one, thus forming a complete circle that started moving around in a procession that had neither a beginning nor an end.

The naturalist expected that after a while the caterpillars would catch on to the joke — get tired of their useless march and start off in some new direction.

But not so.

Through sheer force of habit, the living, creeping circle kept moving around the rim of the pot — around and around, keeping the same relentless pace for seven days and seven nights — and doubtless would have continued longer had it not been for sheer exhaustion and ultimate starvation.

An ample supply of food was close at hand, and plainly visible, but it was outside the range of the circle so the caterpillars continued along the beaten path. They were following instinct, habit, custom, tradition, precedent, past experience, standard practice or whatever you may choose to call it, but they were following blindly.

They mistook activity for accomplishment. They meant well — but they got nowhere.

"Among the chief worries of today's business executives is the large number of unemployed still on the payrolls."

What are the steps you, as an individual, should take in the PBM process?

The 8 Basic Steps

1. Define your key result areas.

2. Determine how to measure success in each area.

3. Take stock of your present performance in each area using the measurement indicators chosen.

4. Prepare a list indicating the level of performance you are ready to commit yourself to.

5. To avoid getting "hung out to dry," negotiate all the above with your immediate superior.

6. Monitor progress as the weeks go by.

7. Review performance with your superior at least quarterly.

8. Summarize the year's results at the end of the year in a review session with your boss as the basis for starting the entire cycle over again the following year.

> *"Those who don't know what they are trying to accomplish will fail. Worse yet, they frequently communicate their uncertainty to others. The result is group ineffectiveness."*

Results are what we need. If we just circle the rim of the pot, the organization and our careers will have a fate similar to that of the caterpillars! Let's concentrate on ...

The Concept of Key Result Areas

What is a "Key Result Area?"

A prevailing attitude among many persons who hesitate or refuse to commit themselves to objectives is the belief that "You can't measure my work." You hear this especially from those who deal with intangibles, with values or with services, as opposed to those whose jobs involve more immediately visible results (manufactured items, dollars, building, etc.).

We believe it is probably more true to say that **some jobs are more difficult to measure than others, but measurement is not impossible.** The difficulty is reduced greatly when we realize that it is difficult to measure any job in its entirety. We shouldn't try to measure the whole job of any one individual, rather, we should break it down into its components. We itemize the separate responsibilities or duties the job entails, those discrete parts of the job we call key result areas. They are not goals, but they are areas of concern we turn into goals. They become goals when we determine how to measure them and add a precise level of accomplishment (or change). But before we measure, we must know what we are trying to measure. A key result area, then, is the answer to the questions, "What is it I am trying to measure?" "What are the things I am accountable for?" and "What are the major component parts of my job?"

Goals on Your Job

Some of your time is spent on repetitive, routine, regular, recurring bread-and-butter operational concerns. These are the normal work outputs of you and your group. Objectives covering these responsibilities are called routine objectives.

Part of your time is also spent on solving problems. When you are result-oriented, problems concern not just the unpleasant items, obstacles or interruptions on the job, but also the outputs with which you are dissatisfied. Problems concern those key result areas where performance is currently not

Results

meeting a satisfactory norm.

Finally, part of your time is spent on developmental, innovative areas, things you are doing because of their long-term impact on your operation. They deal with change that could mean some new product you're getting into for the first time, some new way of doing an old project, some unique program that is understood to be a one-shot deal. You're engaged in these areas, because they add to the results of you and your work group. We call these your innovative objectives. They are the exact opposite of the routine objectives.

The goals we set are based on the kinds of job concerns we have. There is another consideration — the management theory that as one moves from one type of goal to another, the manager climbs an ascending ladder of excellence.

The manager who simply takes care of routine areas of responsibility has the repetitive things under control and runs a tight ship. This manager is worth something to the organization and is valued.

Worth more to the organization though, is the manager who isn't flustered when things go a little out of control. He or she actually expects this occasionally and is wise in finding ways to solve problems as they arise. We usually try to have people around who can do this in their own area of responsibility and in others' areas too, if needed.

Worth still more is the individual who not only controls routine affairs and solves problems as they arise (both of which deal with the present), but who also looks to the future — a person who is developmental, innovative, creative. We prize people who are out there in the foreground, helping forge new frontiers, making the breakthrough for which everyone has been searching.

The challenge in supervision goes beyond routine into the areas of problem-solving and being innovative. The caution here is that one cannot afford to work with the problems and innovations until the routine areas are first under control. Start with the routine result areas — define acceptable standards for them first — get them under control, and then you can delegate them to someone else, while you turn your attention to the problems and innovations.

> *"Obstacles are those frightful things you see when you take your eyes off the goal."*
> Hannah More

100

How to Think About Job-Related Goals

Mission/Role	Organizational Position	Job Description

KEY RESULT AREAS
that are either:

Routine	Problem	Innovative
What is your group's normal work output?	What are the norms for your group's work output?	What new ideas does your group plan to work on?
What are the measurable units or aspects for each output?	In which areas is performance currently not up to these standards?	What will be the measurable or added benefits?
How many units of this output will be required this period?	How much measurable improvement is realistic this period?	What will be the costs to generate these benefits?
Consider using a range to describe the outputs.	What action steps will be taken to remedy the situation?	What steps can be monitored as time goes by?

101

Categories and Classes of Goals

There are two main types of goals: personal and job-related. The wise manager determines his or her goals in both categories because they are interrelated. Here is an outline of the concerns and commitment involved in each classification.

Job-Related Goals

Category One: Job-Related Goals

Class	What It Concerns	Type of Commitment
1. Routine (Regular)	Normal work output	To meet standards
2. Problem-solving	Results below par	To find a solution
3. Innovative	Something new (change)	Added benefits

Personal Development Goals

Category Two: Personal Development Goals

Class	What It Concerns	Type of Commitment
4. Technical/Professional Growth	Information, attitudes, skills	Effort to meet a need
5. Managerial Development	Information, attitudes, skills	Effort to meet a need
6. Growth as a Person	Information, attitudes, skills	Effort to meet a need

To move in the direction essential for your success, your objectives must meet the following three criteria:

1. They Must Be Realistic — Can they be achieved within a reasonable length of time? What costs are involved? Will they bring about desired changes?

2. They Must Be Specific — Do they specify when results can be expected? Do they say what benefits or improvements will be achieved? Do they state what results are sought?

3. They Must Ensure Improvement — Do they offer sufficient challenge? Will they overcome problems, seize opportunities? Do they offer the chance to be of service to others?

Workable Individual Goals
Individual Goals Should:

- Flow from the position description: up, down and across.

- Be consistent with and take their cue from overall organizational goals.

- Be measurable, using appropriate yardsticks or standards.

- Be challenging in order to provide motivation and a feeling of real accomplishment.

- Be attainable and reasonably within the control of the individual.

- Be limited initially — after time, managers can handle more goals effectively.

- Be weighted in order of importance.

- Be guides to action — state what, not how.

- Be reviewed periodically at appropriate and realistic milestones.

- Provide the basis for performance appraisal.

A sample job description follows on the next two pages. Then a clean copy is provided for you to write a Performance-Based Management job description. These are powerful tools in the hands of a person who "thinks like a manager."

> *"If you can't see where you're going, you may not like where you end up."*

Job Description

	Date	Signature
☐ Original		
☒ Revised		
☐ Review/No Change		
☒ Reevaluation		
Requested		

Food Service

Department

2208	Dining Room Supervisor
Job Number	**Title**

POSITION SUMMARY: Write a brief summary highlighting the general function of the position.

Supervises the serving of food on two hot lines, Dining Room, preparation and serving of food at Snack Bar and dishwashing procedures to maintain high standards of sanitation and service throughout the Dining Room, as well as maintaining cash flow by controlling change fund .

TYPICAL RESPONSIBILITIES/DUTIES: List in order of importance. Please use this form only— additional space is provided on the reverse side.

ORDER	TYPE OF ACTIVITY: Starting with an action word, give a brief, concise explanation of what is done.	REASON: Why is this activity performed?	TIME: % of Working Time
1	Supervise and assign daily duties to personnel, and communicate frequently with employees for job performance on all 3 serving areas, Snack Bar, dishroom, cashiers and all daily meetings in the 7 meeting rooms and all food deliveries.	To maintain high efficiency of service to all customers.	50%
2	Order daily from Food Supply for the 24-hr. shift and compose weekly order for General Store-room as well as outside vendors.	To stock adequate amount of supplies needed to assure sufficient service for 7 days a week, 24 hrs. day.	05%
3	Supervise cash flow by counting change fund daily, ordering and counting change bought from bank, relieving and/or filling vacancy of cashiers, operating extra register through peak periods and assist with preparation of daily cashier recap.	To assure accuracy of cash flow.	10%
4	Orient, train, evaluate and discipline as well as adjust any employee grievance. Reschedule or change schedule if necessary in case of absence or illness so as to have coverage for a 24-hour period.	Morale.	05%
5	Supervise and help with all special functions, including stocking of table cloths and napkins, ordering of microphone when needed and prior set-up, service and clean-up of daily meetings in the 7 areas of Dining Room, meetings through-out all buildings.	To give employees, administration of hospital and other groups a comfortable and attractive meeting place with efficient service.	20%

ORDER	TYPE OF ACTIVITY	REASON	TIME
6	Record daily attendance, absence & tardies of each employee. Twice monthly review all 40 time cards and record overtime. Check equipment and fill out maintenance work orders, then follow through to make sure equipment is working properly.	Records of attendance and hours worked during each pay period are essential. Equip- ment must be in work- ing order for us to perform our duties.	05%
7	Responsible for handling all complaints or follow-ing up on complaints with Manager. Must make immediate decisions regarding customers and own employees. Must be able to supervise entire dining room functions without presence of Man-ager or Department Head.	To maintain high standards of service as well as morale of all customers and employees.	05%

SKILL, QUALIFICATIONS, KNOWLEDGE, ABILITY & PHYSICAL REQUIREMENTS: List specific
minimum requirements to satisfactorily perform this position and the reason for the requirement.

Minimum Education and/or Professional Qualifications Skills	High school graduate.	**Reason:** Must be able to read and write and be able to communicate effectively. Must be able to make change in cashier capacity.
Previous Experience	At least one year experience in food service in supervisory capacity.	
Special - Personal Skills, Qualities, Aptitudes and Physical Requirements	Must be able to communicate effectively, give oral and written instructions. Stands and/or walks most of shift.	Supervisor must make out all meeting sheets, schedules, orders, employee records and be able to relate to employee. Dining Room includes many different areas and supervisor must be in all areas.

SUPERVISION OF OTHERS: List below the number of employees and their position for
which this job provides immediate supervision:

No.	Position	No.	Position	No.	Position
4	Cashiers	4	Dish machine Operators		
13	Dining Room Aides				
6	Short-Order Cooks				

Submitted by: _____ Date _____

Job Description

- ☐ Original
- ☐ Revised
- ☐ Review/No Change
- ☐ Reevaluation
  Requested

Date	Signature

Department

Job Number   **Title**

POSITION SUMMARY: Write a brief summary highlighting the general function of the position.

TYPICAL RESPONSIBILITIES/DUTIES: List in order of importance. Please use this form only—
additional space is provided on the reverse side.

ORDER	TYPE OF ACTIVITY: Starting with an action word, give a brief, concise explanation of what is done.	REASON: Why is this activity performed?	TIME: % of Working Time

ORDER	TYPE OF ACTIVITY	REASON	TIME

SKILL, QUALIFICATIONS, KNOWLEDGE, ABILITY & PHYSICAL REQUIREMENTS: List specific <u>minimum</u> requirements to satisfactorily perform this position and the reason for the requirement.

		Reason:
Minimum Education and/or Professional Qualifications Skills		
Previous Experience		
Special - Personal Skills, Qualities, Aptitudes and Physical Requirements		

SUPERVISION OF OTHERS: List below the number of employees and their position for which this job provides immediate supervision:

No.	Position	No.	Position	No.	Position

Submitted by: _____ Date _____

Now that you have considered various categories of goals and clues for setting them, let's look at a case study. This example concerns job-related goals.

The Buck Stops Where?

Jack Benton, a mechanical engineer, was recently promoted to Supervisor at Pilgrim Laboratories, a medium-sized manufacturer of electromechanical components such as TV tuners, loudspeakers and record-changer assemblies. In this capacity he supervised six people, two of whom were also engineering graduates. The others were three technical assistants plus a clerk/secretary.

One of the responsibilities of Benton's section was to provide product engineering services to one of the main production lines: Three-speed record-changer mechanisms that were sold in large quantity to stereo phonograph manufacturers.

As a result of increasing complaints from the field about jamming, Engineering Manager, Gerald Brickmore, decided that the record-changer gear train needed redesign. He passed the assignment on to Benton at a staff meeting and requested that the job be done as quickly as possible.

Benton called his two engineers together that afternoon and explained the problem. Considerable discussion took place on how the design could be changed and the meeting ended on a cooperative note.

At the end of the week Benton checked with each of his engineers to see how they were coming with the new design. He was disappointed to find that only one man had done anything at all on the project and he had only made some rough sketches on scratch paper.

Benton immediately called another meeting which he opened with the comment:

"Now, look, this job is important — the customer keeps complaining. If those lines get shut down, Brickmore will hit the ceiling. We've got to get this job done right away. Let's get going on it."

The two engineers protested about how busy they were on other projects, then a long discussion again took place on the detailed

C
A
S
E

S
T
U
D
Y

engineering changes needed to prevent the changer mechanism from jamming. After two hours, the meeting broke up with general agreement among the three men on what was required to correct the problem.

Benton had to go out of town for a few days and when he returned, the first thing he did was to check the progress on the record-changer design. He again was dismayed at the lack of effort on what had now become his top-priority project. Everyone in his section was busy but not on the changer problem.

Brickmore had asked him just that morning, "How is that record-changer job going?"

If you were Jack Benton, what would you do?

What Actually Happened

After a lot of thought, the next day Benton called his whole group into his office to discuss the record-changer situation which, in his mind, was becoming a crisis. He explained that the problem was critical and that Brickmore was getting impatient. He stated flatly that the engineering changes had to go to production by the end of the month.

He then itemized on a blackboard the detailed design changes that were needed, based on the technical discussion of the previous two meetings. Some of the changes couldn't be started until other changes were completed. Alongside each task he listed the name of the person responsible and asked for an estimated completion date.

After considerable back and forth discussion, a due date was noted on the blackboard alongside each job. As a result, each person, including Benton himself, ended up with specific assignments and deadlines, which each agreed he could meet. Benton then asked the secretary to type up a schedule and distribute a copy to each individual that afternoon.

Three weeks later, all revised specifications were in on time and sent out to production. The changes apparently corrected the jamming problem as field complaints dropped on the first shipment using the new design.

Brickmore later complimented Benton "on a job well done".

Analysis:

CASE STUDY

Analysis

Benton got no action until he listed, in writing (1) the specific tasks to be done, (2) the people responsible, and (3) definite due dates. This is the key to setting up schedules that will be met. Without this definite commitment of WHAT should be done, WHO should do it and WHEN it should be completed, the likelihood would have been that other jobs would have been done first while the most important job sat waiting.

Schedules for Your Job

Here are some basic questions to help you determine how important setting goals will be in your case. Answer each as honestly as you can.

	YES	NO
1. Are you somehow "too rushed" and busy "putting out fires" to think ahead?	____	____
2. Note below your most urgent assignment. Have you set all necessary deadlines and milestones?	____	____
3. Have you distributed a written timetable to people with appropriate due dates? If not, why not?	____	____
4. When you assign work, do you usually give subordinates a chance to set their own schedules, or at least voice their opinions?	____	____
5. Are you in the habit of setting a due date each time you assign work to someone? How about the last one you handed out?	____	____
6. Think back to the most recent assignment your group completed. Would setting tighter deadlines have speeded things up?	____	____

Now review your answers, do you think you could improve in the area of setting goals?

Personal Development Goals

Once your job-related goals have been established, it will be easier to move on to a suggested course of action that involves your personal development. These are the steps you will take to meet your personal development needs. It is important to be specific about the materials to be studied, the programs to be undertaken, or any of the following possibilities that might be considered:

1. Specific job assignment that will broaden your knowledge or experience, e.g., temporary appointment as an acting supervisor.

2. Reading (books, magazines, reports, research publications, job descriptions, procedures, memos, reports, etc.).

3. Program attendance, workshops, seminars, training courses.

4. Management development programs, spelling out whether a highly concentrated area of one or two topics is needed or whether a broad orientation is better.

5. Programmed instruction.

6. Correspondence courses.

7. Association memberships, professional group activities at either local, regional or national levels.

8. Giving papers, writing articles, any type of publishing.

9. Visiting other organizations.

10. Attendance at meetings within your organization that you wouldn't normally attend.

11. Committee work, especially chairing a group, again stressing the growth aspect of such work.

12. Individual instruction or mentoring, such as a one-to-one relationship as an understudy for a period of time; for example, working very closely for a time with a supervisor/manager.

> *"Even if you are on the right track, you'll get run over if you just sit there."*
> Oliver Wendell Holmes

Worksheet —
Personal Growth Objective

I think I need to improve in:

_____

_____

_____

My reason for this belief; my justification for working in this area is:

_____

_____

_____

My major concern is one of (check one):

☐ knowledge

☐ attitude

☐ ability

This deals with growth in (check one):

☐ my profession

☐ my management career

☐ myself as a total person

Think of one personal development need you have noticed or mentioned to one of your subordinates (or a peer). Work out a plan of action to help meet the need. You might select from the list of 12 examples on page 111. Be precise about what work, what courses, what readings, etc.

Worksheet —
Personal Development Goals

Need:

_____

_____

Commitment to be sought from individual as a
means of meeting the need:

_____

_____

_____

How we can both tell his or her effort has helped meet
the need:

_____

_____

_____

Now it's time to do this for yourself. Identify at least one
developmental need for yourself. Be as specific as you
were with another person.

Need:

_____

_____

Commitment I intend to make as a means of
meeting the need:

_____

_____

_____

How my superior and I can tell whether the effort has
helped me grow:

_____

_____

_____

Worksheet —
Subordinate Growth Objective

Name of individual:

_____

I think this individual needs to improve in:

_____

_____

_____

My reason for this belief, my justification for sharing it is:

_____

_____

_____

_____

My major concern for this individual is (check one):

☐   knowledge

☐   attitude

☐   ability

This deals with growth in (check one):

☐   profession

☐   management

☐   total person

Now copy this page and complete it for each of the
people you supervise.

Why PBM Bogs Down

1. Lack of commitment by the CEO and/or top management.

2. Autocratic behavior by the CEO toward installation, e.g., "We're going to have new performance standards. Here are yours." In other words, the objectives are not participatively set.

3. Failure to negotiate on performance-range indicators between bosses and subordinates.

4. Assignment of full responsibility for installation to staff functions, usually personnel or controller's departments or an "Assistant to _____," without further commitment by top management.

5. An assumption by top management that PBM is primarily a tool for training managers and not a framework for decision-making and problem-solving or a management system.

6. Resistance at lower management levels because it is perceived by them as another paperwork project.

7. Fear at lower management levels that PBM will jeopardize existing management information systems or at least not be compatible with existing operational data.

8. Fear by many employees that PBM is a disguised performance review technique.

9. An assumption that budgeting and financial controls are identical to PBM.

10. An assumption that PBM is something radically new and untested.

11. An assumption that PBM will be introduced with a minimal effort and within a short time frame.

12. The introduction of PBM at middle management levels without support by top management.

13. The assumption by CEOs that PBM is fine for subordinates, but their own objectives could not be reduced to writing nor could their performance be evaluated through PBM methodology.

14. An assumption by staff personnel that their work is unmeasurable.

15. General lack of training, feedback, regular reviews and commensurate compensation.

When Performance-Based Management (PBM) Doesn't Work...

- Management isn't committed.

- Goals are not participatively set.

- Supervisors aren't well trained.

- Feedback is missing.

- Reviews aren't conducted regularly.

- Linkage is poor between performance and compensation.

Similarly, these types of errors may also appear:

The Most Common Errors in Goal-Setting

1. The manager doesn't clarify common objectives for the whole unit.

2. Goals set too low to challenge a subordinate.

3. Prior results not used as a basis to find new and unusual combinations.

4. Unit's common objectives not blended with those of the larger unit of which it is part.

5. Individuals overloaded with inappropriate or impossible goals.

6. Responsibilities not clustered in the most appropriate positions.

7. Two or more individuals are allowed to believe themselves responsible for doing exactly the same things.

8. Methods (how) stressed rather than clarifying individual area of responsibility.

9. Emphasis placed on pleasing the boss rather than achieving the job objective.

10. No policies as guides to action — boss waits for results, then issues ad hoc judgments in correction.

11. No probing to discover what subordinate's program for goal achievement will be. Every goal accepted uncritically without a plan for successful achievement.

12. Boss too reluctant to add own (or higher management's) known needs to the program of subordinates.

13. Real obstacles that will face the subordinate are ignored, including many emergency or routine duties that consume time.

14. Proposed new goals or ideas for subordinates are ignored and boss imposes only those that he or she wants.

15. Boss doesn't think through and act upon what he or she must do to help subordinate succeed.

16. Intermediate target dates (milestones) by which to measure progress of subordinate are not set.

17. No new ideas introduced from outside the organization, thereby freezing the status quo.

18. Failure to permit new goals in place of stated objectives that are less important.

19. Failure to discard previously agreed-upon goals that have subsequently proven unfeasible, irrelevant or impossible.

20. Failure to reinforce successful behavior when goals are achieved.

> *"Work is the rent you pay for the room you occupy on earth."*
> Elizabeth, the Queen Mother

Success with PBM is not guaranteed. It requires awareness of several precautions, restrictions and restraints.

Precautions for Implementation of PBM

1. Though not difficult to understand, it requires perseverance — often three to five years for significant benefits.
2. Proficiency requires continuous learning and reinforcement.
3. Managers must differentiate between activities and results, between efficiency and effectiveness, between ineffective activity and accomplishment.
4. Some people prefer not to press for participative management and are more successful as authoritarians.
5. The negotiation of goals in jointly held areas of responsibility, if avoided, will cause the system to fail.

Restrictions

1. Benefits are lost if it is viewed as a means of "tightening the screws" to get more production without regard to the effect on employees.
2. The paperwork can become burdensome and unjustified unless goals and success indicators are carefully prepared and limited in number.
3. Training is needed continuously to help people cope with new situations.
4. Performance based on goals should be appraised continuously — not just at officially designated intervals.

Restraints

1. Supervisors must initiate action. Little happens unless they do.
2. PBM requires joint goal-setting and agreement on key results expected and measures of progress.
3. Emphasis is on the "whats" more than the "hows"; for many experienced managers, this is a difficult discipline.

4. PBM stresses "up-front" negotiation and commitment when risks are greater because less is known.

When you have realistically assessed the precautions and possible problems you will be much better prepared to achieve benefits because:

PBM Combats Management Inertia

Which Exists When:

—Planning and goals are not well understood.

—Jobs are not defined in terms of key results.

—Continued learning of management skills and self-development is limited.

—Decision-making is not delegated and decentralized.

—Accountabilities are unclear.

—Information is lacking for effective problem-solving.

This means there will be these advantages for both supervisors and subordinates.

For Supervisors:

1. Basis for continuing communication.

2. Better interpersonal relationships based on performance factors.

3. Increased options for motivating subordinates.

4. More accurate appraisal.

5. Improved results.

For Subordinates:

1. Authority and accountability clarified.

2. Participation in setting goals and performance standards.

3. Aware of results expected.

4. Can relate personal satisfaction (or lack of it) to job performance.

5. Assured of regular feedback.

> *"Common sense is the knack of seeing things as they are, and doing things as they ought to be done."*
> Stowe

Summary

To summarize, here is why the Performance-Based Management System can provide significant benefits:

- Management development begins with a system to ensure regular communication between bosses and subordinates based on performance.

- You'll never see what you did or did not achieve without objectives.

- We're making these decisions anyway — the challenge is to make them better.

- We must make discriminatory judgments in favor of excellence.

- By checking and defining areas of responsibility we get at the source of future problems and take steps to correct them rather than trying to trace blame.

- Stigma of poor performance tends to remain higher when appraisals are informal or unwritten than when formalized and recorded over a period of time.

- End results of goals are specific, but ways of getting there are left open.

- The faintest ink is better than the finest memory.

Questions for Personal Development

1. What is the major emphasis of this chapter?

2. What do you feel are the most important things you learned from this chapter?

    1)

    2)

    3)

3. How can you apply what you learned to your current job?

    1)

    2)

    3)

4. What objectives will you set to improve? By when (date)?

    1)

    2)

    3)

5. Who can help you most in applying what you learned in this chapter?

6. What are the major roadblocks you expect that may hinder your progress in applying what you learned in this chapter?

    Roadblock　　　　　**Why?**

    1)

    2)

    3)

7. How will you communicate the most important points in this chapter to your key people?

8. What preparation is necessary for this introduction?

9. What changes do you expect to make that will achieve greater motivation of your team?

Change   **By when (date)?**
1)

2)

3)

10. How will you monitor to assure performance has improved, i.e., increased productivity? (Reports, meetings, etc.)

11. What work-related problems concern you most in evaluating how you will benefit from this chapter?

12. Once you've accomplished several milestones, how will you continue developing new ideas and objectives related to this chapter?

13. How would you summarize the change you expect to see in yourself one year from now as a result of what you learned in this chapter?

*C*HAPTER 5

How to Gain and Retain Good People

No doubt about it. Gaining and retaining good people is a top priority and management responsibility. Finding the right people and helping them improve gets easier when managers follow a performance-based approach to interviewing and hiring rather than a task-oriented approach.

Performance-based hiring involves more than asking questions that help you determine how a candidate will perform once hired. It also involves determining how the open position fits into the overall mission and performance goals of the department, identifying the specific results the person will be expected to generate and following an interviewing process that will help you differentiate between candidates and make the best hiring decision every time.

This chapter will:
- Describe how to avoid three mistakes new managers frequently make during the hiring process.
- Help you create an effective, performance-based hiring process.
- Provide a candidate-comparison worksheet to help you differentiate between candidates.
- Offer guidelines for handling a new hire who doesn't perform as well as expected.
- Describe eight steps to help you retain good employees.

How to Avoid Three Common Hiring Mistakes

The three most common mistakes managers make in hiring are:

- Inadvertently putting themselves and their companies at risk by failing to do a thorough job of their pre-interviewing homework.

- They fill the position because it's open, not because it's vital.

- They hire their third, fourth or fifth choice candidate rather than begin a new search when their top two candidates turn down the offer.

How can these mistakes be avoided? Let's explore why it's important to do your pre-interviewing homework, fill the vital position, not the open one and start over if your top two candidates say "no" to the offer.

Do Your Pre-interviewing Homework

The process of interviewing and hiring people often brings new managers face-to-face with critical aspects of business that they didn't have to know before they became managers — such realities as anti-discrimination laws and the current enforcement policies of the Equal Employment Opportunity Commission. While most companies don't expect managers to be legal experts, they do expect managers to learn and follow approved interviewing and hiring guidelines, policies and practices. So, before you conduct an interview, do your homework — thoroughly. Review the information before every interview to make sure it's fresh in your mind.

Five Hiring Steps

Here are five ideas that will help you follow approved interviewing and hiring guidelines, policies and practices:

1. In many but not all companies, the human resources department is the overseer of employee-related policies and procedures. So start your homework there. Ask your human resources department or the person who deals with these issues at your company for general interviewing and hiring dos and don'ts and for any specific rules that apply to your department.

2. In addition to the employees' handbooks, which all employees are given at the time of hire, some companies give new managers a manager's handbook. It details how to handle everything from interviewing and hiring to specific performance problems to termination to rewarding excellence. If you were given a manager's handbook, be sure to follow the interviewing and hiring procedural advice it contains. If you weren't, check to see if one exists.

"Success and failure have the same root- desire to achieve. Avoiding failure is not the same as success."
Dr. Roger Fritz, President, Organization Development Consultants

Questions about anti-discrimination laws and the current enforcement policies of the Equal Employment Opportunity Commission can now be directed to agency experts through a nationwide, free information hotline. Dial (800) USA-EEOC.

3. Remember that it may not be what you ask but how you ask it that makes the legal difference during interviews. So, write down the questions you want to ask candidates and what specifically you're trying to find out through each question. Then ask your human resources department or the person who deals with these issues at your company to review and "okay" the questions. Do this well in advance of the interview; the questions might need to be run by the executive committee or corporate attorney — and that could take some time. Once you've received approval, ask the questions exactly as they were approved.

4. Ask what kind of documentation you should keep to verify that you followed approved interviewing and hiring practices for every candidate. Then, keep that documentation. It can make a critical difference if a candidate challenges your interviewing methods or hiring decision.

5. Ask what the probationary period, if any, is for new employees, what records you need to keep during that period and how termination procedures work during and after the probationary period. The goal isn't to plan for failure; it's to know your management options before you need them just in case that "perfect new employee" turns out to be the "imperfect choice."

Fill the Vital Position, Not the Open One

Filling the vital position instead of merely an open one will help your department accomplish its mission and goals. An open position is the job just vacated — customer service representative, administrative assistant, accounts payable clerk, etc. Traditional hiring involves dusting off the old job description, announcing the opening and hiring a replacement — without first assessing whether or not the position is still vital to the department's mission and goals. If your department has gone through or is going through restructuring or other changes, chances are pretty strong that positions — or at the very least, position descriptions — need updating to reflect department changes. The title of the position may remain the same; however, the job focus and the "must have" credentials in new employees may need to shift to keep the position relevant to the department's goals and the organization's mission.

Example — The Case of Changing Job Responsibilities:

A customer service department that has never been responsible for negotiating renewal contracts with established clients is suddenly given that responsibility by the executive committee. In the past, good communication skills and technical knowledge were the "must have" skills for customer service representatives. Now, however, the new responsibility of negotiating renewal contracts means negotiation skills are now top priority for all customer service representatives. While the job title of customer service representative remains the same, the focus of the job description and the "must have" credentials for this position must be updated if the new employee is to accomplish the vital responsibility of successfully negotiating renewal contracts with established clients. Moreover, current customer service representatives must be trained in negotiating.

> *"Failure is determined by what you allow to happen... Success by what you make happen."*
> Dr. Roger Fritz, President, Organization Development Consultants

127

Start Over if Your Top Two Candidates Say "No" to Your Offer

You've followed a carefully designed, performance-based interviewing process — one that took into consideration the department's mission and goals and the results the person will be held accountable for producing — and you've ranked every candidate according to skills and experience. Of all the candidates interviewed, two stand out because they have the "must have" skills and experiences identified as being most important to the position. Choosing between the two candidates is hard, but you do. You extend an offer to your first-choice candidate, who says "no." So, you extend the offer to your second-choice candidate, who also says "no." Now what do you do?

Proceed with extreme caution. If you don't, you'll turn the performance-based interviewing process you so carefully followed into the task-oriented goal of filling a position fast. And, if that happens, you'll probably make a hiring mistake.

Before you offer the position to the candidate you ranked as number three, four or five, stop and think. Ask yourself if hiring this candidate fulfills a short-term plan to fill the position fast or a long-term plan to fill the position with the best person for the job. Be brutally honest. When you're feeling pressured to hire fast, it's easy to justify offering the job to less-qualified (perhaps even unqualified) candidates.

Example — The Case of the Medical Miss-Hire:

A successful medical staff recruiter was promoted to manager. As manager, her first challenge was to hire a new recruiter to fill the position she had vacated. The manager identified the qualifications necessary for a medical recruiter's success: excellent telephone communication skills, especially the ability to build rapport fast; discovering how the person decides; a flexible, friendly, professional approach; and experience in the health care industry. The manager interviewed dozens of candidates. Her first- and second-choice candidates, who met all the qualifications, turned down the job offer. Rather than starting over, the manager offered the position to candidate number three, even though that candidate had a stiff and formal communication style, no selling experience and very little knowledge of the medical industry. Candidate number three accepted the job. Within two weeks of hiring the inexperienced, underqualified recruiter, the manager knew she had hired a good person for the wrong job. She checked with the human resources department to find out her options and discovered that to replace the new recruiter would require a great deal of her time, reams of documentation and would probably take several months. At that point she would start over, reposting the position and going through the interviewing and hiring process again. Her hiring decision proved to be an expensive mistake in every way — time, effort and money.

> *"Every great mistake has a halfway moment, a split second when it can be recalled and perhaps remedied."*
> Pearl S. Buck

You can learn from this manager's experience. If the candidates ranked number three or lower didn't have enough of the "must have" skills and credentials to make the top of your preferred-candidates list, before you make them a job offer ask yourself, "So, what's changed?" Accept the fact that the top two candidates said "no."

Managers are usually better off starting over with the hiring process if the top two candidates refuse the job offer. Starting over means reassessing everything — including the reasons the candidates turned down the offer. For instance, if they turned it down because of compensation, compare the costs of offering them a more attractive package with the costs of readvertising, interviewing, being short-staffed, etc. A comprehensive reassessment will help you determine whether it is wiser to make one of your top two candidates another offer or to spend the time and money readvertising and interviewing for the position.

> *"Failure is the only opportunity to more intelligently begin anew."*
> Henry Ford

Performance-Based Hiring

Experienced managers know that one of the best ways to retain a good workforce is to hire the right people into jobs that match their skills and interests. Performance-based interviewing and hiring help you do just that. The clearer you are about the positions you are filling, the easier it will be to develop and follow a performance-based interviewing and hiring process that helps you make the best hiring decisions every time.

129

Six Steps to Performance-Based Interviewing and Hiring

Step One: Identify interviewing criteria

Before you begin screening applicants, identify the criteria that will help you determine which applicants are or aren't qualified to become candidates for the position you're filling.

Chapter Four, **Performance-Based Management**, described how to develop a job description that prioritizes job activities, discussed why this activity was important and described the amount of work time that should be devoted to each activity. These are all important first steps in preparing yourself for screening applicants and interviewing candidates.

So first, look at the job description for the position you want to fill and, before you do anything else, identify the credentials and skills that are critical to that position. These credentials and skills become the "Success Factors" on the Candidate Comparison Worksheet that follows and that you will use to help differentiate between candidates during the interview process. It will also help you build consistent documentation about the interviewing process and the hiring decision you make.

There is room to write in 10 success factors on this sheet. (Be sure to ask your human resources department for feedback to ensure that the criteria you've identified meet Equal Employment Opportunity Commission and anti-discriminatory regulations.) Underneath each success factor, indicate how important it is to the overall performance of the job. If it's a "must have," weight it a 10. If it's a "preferred but not a must," weight it a five. If it's "not important," weight it a one.

If you've weighted all or most of the factors as "10s," go back and prioritize. If you've weighted all or most of the factors as "fives," check to see that the really important credentials are listed as "10s." If you've weighted all or most of the factors as "ones," take another look at the job itself — why does it exist if the success factors aren't important?

Leave enough space in the "Candidates" column to put the names of all the people you interview after the initial screening. Notice that, after you score the candidates according to the success factors, you'll rank them in order of preference — with plenty of space for comments that will later trigger your memory of why you ranked each candidate the way you did.

CANDIDATE COMPARISON WORKSHEET

Job Title: _____ Date: _____

						Success Factors					Notes
Weight Factor Scale 1 ..... Not important 5 ..... Prefer to have 10 ..... Must have											
WEIGHT											
CANDIDATES											

Candidates ranked in order	Score	Comments
1.		
2.		
3.		
4.		
5.		

Final Choice
1.
2.
3.

Notes:

☐ We're okay ☐ Review ☐ Action needed ☐ Person responsible

IS THE CANDIDATE A GOOD MATCH?
Job Testing

Testing of skills, knowledge, potential and honesty is necessary. However, any test that causes an adverse impact on women, minorities or other protected groups must be formally validated as job related. Validation procedures can be complicated and expensive.

131

Step Two: Evaluate and Screen Applicants

Now that you've prepared your Candidate Comparison Worksheet, you're ready to begin evaluating and screening the applicants.

You've established job "must-have" requirements. These become automatic "knockouts" during the screening process.

Quickly scan all resumes for knockouts and put them in pile number one. Put the resumes that meet *some* of your must-have criteria in pile number two and put the resumes that seem to meet *all* of your must-have criteria in pile number three. Then, go through the resumes in pile number three (people who seem to meet all of your must-have requirements) and pile number two (people who meet some of your must-have requirements), again looking for a match between each applicant and the job requirements in these areas:

1. Work history
2. Education/training
3. Patterns of stability
   (staying a reasonable length of time on each job)
4. Upward movement, promotion, money, responsibility
5. Participation in professional and community activities
6. Leadership positions
7. Accomplishments/results achieved

Establish an order for interviewing the applicants who appear to meet all of or some of your must-have criteria. It's sad, but true: You just can't tell by the resume. You'll want to verify all the credentials and job history and check references to be sure the applicants have accurately described themselves.

Step Three: Screen by Telephone

Before the applicants are interviewed in person, conduct mini-interviews by telephone. The benefits are:

- Telephone mini-interviews are fast, objective and save considerable time and expense.

- Telephone interviews are especially important screening devices if you're filling a position involving a high percentage of telephone work (telemarketing, customer service, executive secretary, etc.). People often do not communicate the same on the phone as they do in person. So, to more accurately assess their telephone skills, "test them" at least once.

- Another approach is to consider placing an employment ad that encourages all applicants to "call only" (before sending a resume) on certain days between certain hours. Remember: As you talk with each applicant, inform him or her that you are taking telephone applications. Ask specific questions that help you determine if the applicant meets your "must-have" and "preferred" criteria. Remember to fill out the Candidate Comparison Worksheet as you go.

- As soon as you know an applicant doesn't match your requirements, discontinue the mini-interview by thanking the person for calling and mark your worksheet: "Rejected—does not meet 'must-have' requirements."

- Ask applicants who meet your requirements to follow up with resumes or schedule interviews.

Step Four: Interview the Candidates

Any test that causes an adverse impact on women, minorities or other groups must be formally validated as job related. Validation procedures can be complicated and expensive.

- Ask every candidate the same questions in the same order to make your documentation, weighting and ranking processes easier. Be sure to check with the human resources department for question-asking dos and don'ts before you interview anyone.

- Ask closed-ended questions to verify information on the resume or from the telephone mini-interview. Closed-ended questions are questions phrased to generate a "yes-or-no" answer.

- Ask open-ended or performance-based questions to discover how candidates are likely to respond in the situations they will face on the job. Open-ended questions are questions that are designed to get descriptive answers, not "yes" or "no" answers. Descriptive answers are your best indicators of how the candidate is likely to think and behave once hired. Be sure the open-ended questions you ask are designed to help you see how the candidate would use "must have" and "preferred" qualities like negotiation or problem-solving skills. Questions beginning with "What would you do if....," "Tell me about a team challenge you were involved in and how you helped resolve it," and "Describe the most difficult negotiation you've experienced and how you resolved it successfully" will generate valuable information to help you differentiate between candidates who, on paper, seem to meet all your "must-have" credentials and those who, in reality, do not.

- Testing of skills, knowledge and attitude can be very useful but should be handled carefully.

Step Five: Rank the Candidates and Make an Offer to the Top One

If that candidate turns down the offer, approach your second-choice candidate. If that candidate says "no," refer to the advice given earlier — carefully weigh the benefits of starting over with the potential costs of hiring a candidate who doesn't have the right qualifications.

The best approach is to follow the performance-based interviewing process and extend an offer only to the candidates whose qualifications and skills match the specific job requirements.

The true test of the match between candidate and position begins on the first days of employment. And, the first days on the job can leave you and your new employee questioning the decision or looking forward to a mutually-rewarding, long-term business relationship. So it is as important for you to form a plan for the employee's first days on the job as it is to plan an effective performance-based interviewing strategy. Here's how.

Step Six: Start with Enthusiasm

New employees, no matter how skilled, appreciate the performance-based manager who takes the time to sit down and help them identify the major task and behavior goals they are expected to accomplish during the probationary period, usually the first three months of employment.

One of the most effective ways to accomplish this is to schedule a two or three hour period to talk and identify in writing what needs to be done or learned first, how efforts will be measured and feedback about results achieved.

Set regular meetings with the new employee to review progress. This will help you determine if the employee is on track or if problems are occurring. The goal is to do everything possible to ensure a new employee's success and to turn any problems around before they become too serious to fix.

> *If you don't know where you're going, any road will take you there.*

What to Do if the New Employee Doesn't Perform as Expected

Before doing anything, check with the human resources department to ensure that you follow your organization's preferred methods and timelines for handling non-performers. These four steps serve only as guidelines to familiarize you with the general process. The best place to get specific information about how to handle non-performers is from your organization or from the professionals they refer you to.

Step One: Hold an Appraisal Meeting

If at any time after agreeing on specific goals and measurement methods, you discover that your new employee isn't doing what he or she agreed to do, immediately schedule a meeting to appraise the situation. Use the following chart as your discussion guide to determine the causes and reaffirm commitment to the goals and timelines for achieving them. Since this is your first meeting, make all comments in the appraisal column.

Thirteen Reasons People Don't Do What They're Supposed to Do...

	Appraise	Discipline	Terminate
1. They don't know they should do it.			
2. They don't know how to do it.			
3. They don't know what they are supposed to do.			
4. They think your way will not work.			
5. They think their way is better.			
6. They think something else is more important.			
7. There is no positive outcome to them for doing it.			
8. They think they are doing it.			
9. They are rewarded for not doing it.			
10. They are punished for doing it.			
11. They anticipate negative consequences.			
12. No negative consequence exists for poor attempts.			
13. Obstacles exist that exceed their control.			

Adapted from *Why Employees Don't Do What They're Supposed to Do and What to Do About It*. Ferdinand Fournies, Liberty House Press, 1988.

Step Two: Hold a Positive Disciplinary Meeting

If, after this appraisal meeting, you do not see the required change in behavior, take a positive approach to discipline by following these guidelines:

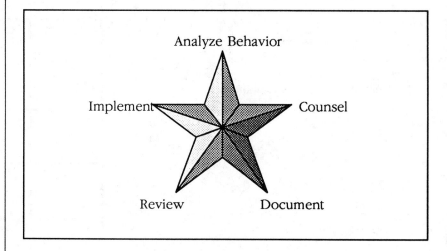

Step Three: Document

You may want to document this meeting just in case the employee's behavior still doesn't change and you have to take stronger action. Before documenting unacceptable performance or behavior, be sure you understand the entire situation. After you have investigated the incident or behavior, use the following as a checklist for preparing your warning letter:

- Be sure the letter is neat and readable.

- Address the letter to the employee. Be sure the preparer of the document dates and signs it.

- Always clearly describe the specific details — who, what, where, why, when, how — in the letter.

- Avoid subjective statements and emphasize association policies and procedures.

- Offer solutions and state objectives and time-lines for accomplishing them.

- Spell out the consequences of continued poor performance, for example, ..."failure to...will result in further disciplinary action up to and including termination."

Step Four: Conduct a Termination Interview

1. Do your homework.

2. If the situation seems to call for it, have a "friendly witness" present during the session.

3. Give clear, specific reasons for the termination. Put them in writing, signed by both parties.

4. Help the employee realize that once the consequences were explained, continuing the unsatisfactory behavior was the employee's responsibilty.

5. The focus of the termination is on unacceptable behavior, not the person.

6. If it is applicable, advise the employee of the implications of removing files, equipment or other organizational property, as well as revealing trade secrets to competitors.

7. Not all employees will take termination calmly, although the termination should come as no surprise. Should the employee become upset, these steps will help:
    a. Listen.
    b. Share.
    c. Continue.
    d. Above all, stay in control of your own emotions. There's no need for you to feel threatened by words — you still work there.
    e. If you are physically threatened and there is no one with you, call in someone else immediately.

8. Know your company policies.

9. Let employees know where they stand with you. Will you provide references? A final word: Your anxiety about the termination session is both normal and healthy — it is a sign that you are a caring, feeling person, involved with a difficult task.

10. Help employees realize that termination is painful for everyone; you and the organization would like everyone to succeed — and you wish them well.

But, the best plan of all is to do everything in your power to prevent an enthusiastic new hire from turning into a disgruntled employee.

Summary

• Hiring and developing the best people you can find is a vital management responsibility.

• To avoid three common hiring mistakes:

1   Do your pre-interviewing homework.
2.   Fill the vital position, not the open one.
3.   Start over if your top two candidates say "no" to your offer.

• Performance-based hiring involves six steps:

1.   Identify interviewing criteria.
2.   Evaluate and screen applicants.
3.   Screen by telephone.
4.   Interview the candidates.
5.   Rank the candidates and make an offer to the top one.
6.   Start with enthusiasm.

• If the new employee doesn't perform as expected, the process usually involves:

1.   Conducting an appraisal meeting
2.   Holding a positive disciplinary meeting
3.   Documentation
4.   Conducting a termination interview

• The best approach with a new employee is one that helps you prevent problem behavior from occurring.

Questions For Personal Development

1. What is the major emphasis of this chapter?

2. What do you feel are the most important things *you* learned from this chapter?

    1)

    2)

    3)

3. How can you apply what you learned to your current job?

    1)

    2)

    3)

4. What objectives will you set to improve? By when (date)?

5. Who can help you most in applying what you learned in this chapter?

6. What major roadblocks may hinder your progress in applying what you learned in this chapter?

Roadblocks   **Why**

1)

2)

3)

7. How will you communicate the most important points in this chapter to your key people?

8. What preparation is necessary to do this?

9. What changes do you expect to make that will achieve greater motivation of your team?

Change	By when (date)?

1)

2)

3)

10. How will you determine that performance has improved, for example, that productivity has increased? (reports, meetings, measurements)

11. What work-related problems concern you most in evaluating how you can benefit from this chapter?

12. How would you summarize the change you expect to see in yourself one year from now as a result of what you learned in this chapter?

*C*HAPTER 6

Delegation

Performance is a word that is becoming increasingly popular in the '90s. In the previous chapter we reviewed the basics of creating and improving performance.

Performance is achieved by individuals or a group of people. The team "captain" doesn't and can't do everything; at times the group must function effectively without its leader. For this to happen, however, decisions must be continuously made about "what to delegate."

Delegation is a tool to align duties for maximum results and, at the same time, avoid overload and burnout.

What to Delegate

Here are four areas where most managers could delegate more. Do you have work that fits in these categories and should be delegated? List items you could delegate in the space provided.

1. Problems or issues that require exploration, study and recommendations for decision.

   Current Examples:

   1.

   2.

   3.

2. Activities that come within the scope of the subordinate's job and abilities.

   Current Examples:

   1.

   2.

   3.

3. Tasks that tap human talent in a positive direction — toward organizational goals and needs and toward the person's development and growth.

   Current Examples:

   1.

   2.

   3.

4. Problems or activities that, if well handled by the subordinate, could conserve the boss's valuable time.

   Current Examples:

   1.

   2.

   3.

Conversely, some things should not be delegated:

After each of the points below, give your reasons why it might not be appropriate to delegate.

1. Planning — setting plans within larger plans and objectives.
   Reason:

2. Morale problems of considerable importance in the work unit.
   Reason:

3. Reconciling differences between line and staff members.
   Reason:

4. Coaching and developing direct subordinates.
   Reason:

5. Reviewing subordinates' performance — one and two levels down.
   Reason:

6. Direct assignment that your boss has given specifically to you to complete.
   Reason:

7. A significant or confidential part of an assignment.
   Reason:

8. Only part of a problem, when you or someone else is already working on the whole problem.
   Reason:

9. Certain "pet" projects, ideas or activities — when these do not cut your larger responsibilities.
   Reason:

10. Matters for which there just isn't enough qualified talent available to delegate to.
    Reason:

What NOT to Delegate

Every manager must make the decision about what to delegate. Consider the following case:

Gibson — The Ultimate Delegator

Gibson was "discovered" by a consultant who was in the process of interviewing managers in a client organization about meetings with their subordinates. The consultant was trying to find out whether subordinates were offered the opportunity to initiate discussion and actively participate in the decision-making process or were merely afforded the opportunity to hear about decisions that had been made.

When asked about regular meetings with subordinates, Gibson said that he met with them for two hours on the same day each week. "My subordinates tell me about the decisions they've made during the past week," he said. He further stated that he really didn't believe in participative decision-making: "No, I don't make their decisions for them, and I just don't believe in participating in the decisions they should be making either; we hold the weekly meeting so that I can keep informed on what they're doing and how."

When a subordinate of Gibson's was interviewed and asked if Gibson made decisions, he answered, "No, he doesn't. Everything he told you is true. He simply does not get involved in decisions that his subordinates are being paid to make. They tell me he plays tennis a great deal in the time he saves." This subordinate was asked if he had ever tried to get Gibson to make a decision. His response was: "Only once. I had been on the job for only about a week when I ran into an operating problem I couldn't solve, so I phoned Gibson. He answered the phone and I told him who I was and that I had a problem. His response was instantaneous: 'Fine, solving problems is what you are being paid for.' When I persisted, he was sharp and suggested that I ask one of the other men to help me with my problem. I didn't know which one to consult and insisted on seeing him. Gibson finally agreed to see me right away. He asked me what my problem was and wrote down my answers. He asked what the conditions for its solution were, and I replied that I didn't understand what he meant. He said, 'If you don't know what conditions have to be satisfied for a solution to be reached, how do you know when you've solved the problem?' He told me he would work out this problem with me this time only, but that it was my job."

Another subordinate of Gibson's was asked about the weekly meetings. He said, "Well, we all sit around that big table in Gibson's office. He just sits there, and we go around the table talking about the decisions we've made, and, if we got help, who helped us. The other guys occasionally make comments — especially if the particular decision being discussed was like one they'd had to make themselves at some point or if it had some direct effect on their own operations." He added that Gibson said very little at most meetings, but that he did pass on any new developments that he had heard about from the main office.

The CEO of Gibson's organization was interviewed and confirmed that Gibson definitely had the most efficient unit. When asked about the turnover rate in Gibson's unit, the CEO said, "There is a pretty big turnover." When asked if the employees couldn't take Gibson's system, the CEO responded, "No, that's not it — most of the people go on to be unit managers themselves. Under Gibson's method of supervision, they are used to working on their own."

At another meeting with Gibson, he was asked about the individual who takes over the weekly meeting when Gibson is gone, and how he chooses the person to fill that slot. He responded, "That's simple. I just pick the person who is most often referred to as the one my subordinates turn to for help in dealing with their problems. Then I try him or her out in this assignment while I'm off. It's good training. Those who can handle it I recommend for any vacancies that come along at the unit manager level. The main office people always contact me for candidates."

All other managers interviewed, except Gibson, either stated explicitly or made it clear during the course of the interviews that important decisions in their meetings were made by themselves. They received suggestions, considered their sources, etc., and then made the final decision. In using this approach to "group decision-making," they made it obvious that they believed that one of the key responsibilities of an upper-level executive is to act as chief decision-maker for those who report to him or her. These managers often believed that it was a joint decision. Their subordinates were likely to feel manipulated if they weren't looking for a way to avoid decision-making and the accompanying risk. Gibson did allow some margin in case emergency action on his part was inevitable, but made it clear that he wanted to hear about problems only after they had been solved and about decisions only after they had been made so that his subordinates couldn't second guess him.

Gibson's overriding concern was with results — the results his subordinates achieved through methods they developed either by themselves or by working with their peers. He simply refused to do their work for them, even at the risk of incurring short-term costs. He put his time and energy into negotiating objectives with subordinates, improving his unit, adapting it to changing environmental conditions and allocating resources for present and future effective.

Gibson is obviously at the far extreme as a delegator. This may or may not be right for you. To help you determine "how much delegating is enough," here is a series of simple questions to assess your situation.

C A S E S T U D Y

> "When you hire people who are smarter than you are, you prove you are smarter than they are."
> R. H. Grant

How Much Delegating Is Enough?

YES   NO

____ ____ Do you often work overtime?

____ ____ Do you take work home evenings and weekends?

____ ____ Is your unfinished work increasing?

____ ____ Are daily operations so time-consuming that you have little time left for planning and other important matters?

____ ____ Do you have control of all details to have a job done right?

____ ____ Do you frequently have to postpone long-range projects?

____ ____ Are you harassed by constant unexpected emergencies?

____ ____ Do you lack confidence in your subordinates' abilities to shoulder more responsibility?

____ ____ Do you find yourself irritable and complaining when the work of your group doesn't live up to expectations?

____ ____ Do conflict, friction and loss of morale characterize the atmosphere of your work group?

____ ____ Do your subordinates defer all decisions to you?

____ ____ Do you instruct your subordinates to perform certain activities, rather than to accomplish certain goals?

____ ____ Have subordinates stopped presenting their ideas to you?

____ ____ Do operations slow down much when you are away?

____ ____ Do you feel that you're abdicating your role as a manager if you ask for your subordinates' assistance?

____ ____ Do you believe that your status and the salary you earn automatically mean that you have to be overworked?

If the majority of your answers are affirmative, it's likely that you're not delegating enough.

Delegation Musts

1. Understand the need for delegation.
The supervisor must understand and agree that delegation is necessary. Subordinates must understand their obligations.

2. Designate goals and objectives.
All parties must understand organizational goals and objectives. There should be general agreement on what is to be done, why, how well, when, in what priority, with what resources and by whom.

3. Know strengths of subordinates.
The supervisor should know the characteristics and capabilities of associates and subordinates and delegate according to their interests and capabilities.

4. Communicate with superiors.
The supervisor should reach an understanding with those above about what is to be redelegated.

5. Negotiate performance standards.
Performance standards must be broad enough to encourage individual initiative, creativity and organizational loyalty. The delegator and the subordinate should agree on them, if possible, in a way that the subordinate can feel he or she is a fully participating member.

6. Agree on areas not to be delegated.
Any exceptions to delegation should be clearly explained by the supervisor and should be understood to be exceptions rather than the rule.

7. Plan for determining skills and training.
Delegation should include the opportunity for testing employees' skills and for providing any necessary training.

8. Show your interest.
The supervisor should show genuine interest in what is being done by subordinates.

9. Measure results.
Results can be assessed in a variety of ways such as: The use of systems of reporting in key result areas, measurement of performance and evaluation of standards of achievement.

10. Offer help and more training.
When tactfully correcting errors, the emphasis should be on target-setting; the employee should have played a part in choosing the targets. Continuous training can bring about self-corrections on the part of employees.

Delegation: My Self-Rating

Poor	Doubtful		Excellent	
1	2	3	4	5
—	—	—	—	—
—	—	—	—	—
—	—	—	—	—
—	—	—	—	—
—	—	—	—	—
—	—	—	—	—
—	—	—	—	—
—	—	—	—	—
—	—	—	—	—
—	—	—	—	—

151

> "Nothing is quite
> as embarrassing
> as watching
> your boss do
> something you
> assured him
> couldn't be
> done."

Knowing all this about delegation won't really help you until you make the decision...

What Will I Delegate?

It boils down to that! So let's try an exercise. Some of the activities listed on the next page may be your routine tasks while others may be entirely out of your realm. That doesn't matter. Your assignment is to decide whether you or your staff should handle each listed task. Consider your total time management program as you make your decisions. There are no correct answers. The purpose is to start you thinking about using your staff to the fullest potential and to encourage you to seriously evaluate your disposition of duties and responsibilities.

> "Never try to teach a pig to
> sing; it wastes your time and
> it annoys the pig."
> Paul Dickson

Would you do the following yourself or delegate it to your staff?

	Do It Myself	Delegate It
1. Represent your unit in routine meetings.	_____	_____
2. Write an interoffice memo.	_____	_____
3. Open and sort today's mail.	_____	_____
4. Brainstorm new ideas.	_____	_____
5. Arrange for temporary help.	_____	_____
6. Read relevant trade journals and books.	_____	_____
7. Handle a personnel problem.	_____	_____
8. Plan an advertising campaign.	_____	_____
9. Talk to a top customer or vendor.	_____	_____
10. Schedule vacations.	_____	_____
11. Handle routine office personnel chores.	_____	_____
12. Work on the unit budget.	_____	_____
13. Submit objectives in your department.	_____	_____
14. Schedule your out-of-town appointments.	_____	_____
15. Hire additional help.	_____	_____
16. Give orientation to a new employee.	_____	_____
17. Be interviewed for a work-related magazine article.	_____	_____
18. Decide on a new intercom system.	_____	_____
19. Arrange for coffee and rolls for a meeting.	_____	_____
20. Follow up on your phone messages.	_____	_____

Take careful notice of the number of responsibilities you would retain for yourself. IS IT REALISTIC?

Try placing beside various tasks on this list the names of your subordinates who could handle the responsibilities.

Summary

If delegating is a new experience for you, don't be over-cautious. Start with basic tasks that are not critical. Work your way up to the point where others are doing everything they can do well and you are performing those managerial functions that you can and should be doing yourself. You will then be managing your subordinates and managing your time as well.

When you fail to delegate effectively, look for the reasons. "Culprits" are likely to include:

- **Lack of patience:** "It takes longer to explain than to do it myself."

- **Insecurity:** Recently promoted managers are often not yet comfortable in their new jobs and can't resist going back to tell their replacement how to proceed.

- **Anxiety:** So eager to "prove themselves" that they refuse to delegate.

- **Inflexibility:** Convinced that nothing can be done properly unless done personally.

- **Inadequacy:** Fear of being shown up.

- **Occupational hobby:** So attached to some aspect of the job that they just don't want to delegate it.

The remedy for effective delegating:

Step I: Recognition of the above "culprits."

Step II: Practicing eliminating them. Delegation is a skill that is learned through practice.

> "*If you pick up a starving dog and make him prosperous, he will not bite you. This is the principal difference between a dog and a man.*"
> Mark Twain

Questions for Personal Development

1. What is the major emphasis of this chapter?

2. What do you feel are the most important things you learned from this chapter?
    1)

    2)

    3)

3. How can you apply what you learned to your current job?
    1)

    2)

    3)

4. What objectives will you set to improve? By when (date)?
    1)

    2)

    3)

5. Who can help you most in applying what you learned in this chapter?

6. What are the major roadblocks you expect may hinder your progress in applying what you learned in this chapter?

    Roadblock   **Why?**
    1)

    2)

    3)

7. How will you communicate the most important points in this chapter to your key people?

8. What preparation is necessary for this introduction?

9. What changes do you expect to make that will achieve greater motivation of your team?

   Change   **By when (date)?**

   1)

   2)

   3)

10. How will you monitor to assure that performance has improved, i.e., productivity has increased? (Reports, meetings, etc.)

11. What work-related problems concern you most in evaluating how you benefit from this chapter?

12. Once you've accomplished several milestones, how will you continue developing new ideas and objectives related to this chapter?

13. How would you summarize the change you expect to see in yourself one year from now as a result of what you learned in this chapter?

*C*HAPTER 7

Improving Performance

From the employer's viewpoint, management development involves being as deliberate and objective as possible about placing the most qualified people in jobs that best match their abilities and accomplishments. From the standpoint of the individual, management development means building and using abilities and skills in order to be advanced on the basis of performance.

While employers must continue to work to strengthen their management development efforts, major responsibility for learning, developing and continuing education rests with the individual manager. If managers do not perceive themselves as leaders, no amount of management development will take root. It is only when individuals decide that management is what they want to do that true management development can begin. It is the individual who must set his or her own goals and seek to have performance measured against those goals.

What is the real key to success in management? It isn't so much what someone else says about you as what you are doing about yourself. This chapter will focus on the continuous process of performance evaluation and self-appraisal as the basis for improvement.

Factors in Management Effectiveness

Effectiveness in management is a career-long process involving eight fundamental factors. The sooner we understand these basic elements and begin to use them, the greater the benefits. Each step is as important as another, and the steps must be "climbed" one at a time.

1. Evaluating results
    - Where have we been?

2. Analyzing needs
    - Where are we now?

3. Setting objectives
    - What should we do?
    - How will progress be measured?
    - What specific indicators will be used?

4. Determining accountability
    - Who will do what by when?

5. Measuring progress
    - How am I doing?
    - How are you doing?
    - How are we doing?

6. Appraising performance
    - How did I do?
    - How did you do?
    - How did we do?

7. Recognizing improvement
    - How will you be rewarded?

8. Projecting the future
    - What must we continue to do?
    - What should we stop doing?
    - What should be changed?

The Individual Manager's Needs

As individuals, we have these five basic needs or expectations of our supervisors. In the same way, these needs are expected of us:

1. "Tell me what you expect from me."
2. "Give me an opportunity to perform."
3. "Let me know how I'm getting along."
4. "Give me guidance where I need it."
5. "Pay and promote me according to my contribution."

Most of the reasons for poor performance are directly related to these needs:

Reasons for Poor Performance

1. Does not know what is expected. (#1 above.)
2. Does not know how he or she is doing. (#3 above.)
3. Cannot do. (A training problem.)
4. Will not do. (An attitude problem.)
5. Lacks organizational support. (#2 above.)
6. Has poor relationship with the boss. (#4 above.)

One of the most important tasks for managers is to eliminate excuses for failure in these areas. How are you doing?

When reviewing the progress of any employee, use:

Four Types of Progress Reviews

1. The Performance Review — manager reviews subordinate's progress and coaches with reference to:

- Work accomplishment as related to previously agreed-upon goals.
- Improvement needed.
- Support needed.

What Do Your Employees Want?

2. The Salary Review — manager reviews:

- The value of results accomplished by the person.
- The relationship of these results to the salary administration program.
- The use of results accomplished as a basis for recommending appropriate salary action.

3. The Career Planning Review — manager counsels subordinates with reference to:

- Interests and aspirations — in relation to employee's future.
- Present **KASH** position of the employee — namely:
  - **K**nowledge and experience.
  - **A**bilities and aptitudes.
  - **S**kills and proficiencies.
  - **H**abits and work relationships.
- Work done—particularly opportunities for improvement.
- Personal development — in terms of a plan and program for growth.

4. The Promotion Review — manager discusses:

- Opportunities that may be available in the future.
- Possible positions — in terms of results required to qualify for them.
- Needed qualifications — in terms of job performance and personal factors.

The subordinate should never be just a bystander in the evaluation process. Neither should the employee's appraisal be filled with surprises. If subordinates have been participating in organizational objectives, unexpected reactions should be minimal. When there is participation we can seriously begin the process of self-appraisal.

The Philosophy of Self-Appraisal

Self-appraisal is a vital key to participative management. When the individuals share the burden of appraisal with superiors, they approach the performance review situation

K
A
S
H

with a significantly different attitude. **When invited, urged and assisted by the procedure to appraise our own performance, our appraisals are colored by the knowledge that we play a vital role in shaping our own destiny.** In actuality, we do, and should assume such a role as a participating member of the management team. The feeling of futility, frustration and antagonism toward the supervisor and the organization experienced in other appraisal systems in which the individual is called in, allowed to read a completed and agreed-upon review, and informed of his or her status — no questions asked or tolerated — is not apt to exist under the philosophy of self-appraisal.

Another aspect of self-appraisal must be recognized. We grow and learn through experience on the job. It is easy, however, to become so involved in the day-to-day process of getting the work out that we have little time or inclination to study and analyze what we have been doing. The self-appraisal element of the performance review forces us to study, analyze and give self-critical attention to the work of the past year. We gain new insights and we continue to grow.

The connotation, possibly through usage related to the labor movement, of the word "negotiation" has become tainted and has been avoided in our discussion of managerial relationships. We can negotiate with each other without animosity, militant aggressiveness or other forms of strife often associated with the word. We are management. We must manage, and negotiation is a management process.

There is no such thing as an easy performance review. It continues to be one of the most difficult responsibilities for all managers. It is, however, one of the most fundamental and potentially most productive of all the manager's many duties. While there is no easy way to approach this job, the philosophy of self-appraisal opens the door to a satisfactory review with a minimum of difficulty.

When objectives have been set by the individual and agreed to by the supervisor, we have laid the groundwork for appraising "results" not "personality traits." If we have gone further and agreed on the relative importance of each objective, we have a stronger basis for evaluation. This type of appraisal measures not only the results we have achieved, but the quality of our objective-setting program, our communications and our ability as a professional manager as well.

> *"I can't afford to die, not when I'm booked."*
> George Burns, after signing a contract to appear at the London Palladium in 1996, when he will be 100.

The Benefits of Self-Appraisal

Self-Appraisal:

— Places the development burden with the individual.

— Answers employees' two most basic questions:

"How am I doing?"

"Where do I go from here?"

— Provides the basis for agreement on priorities.

— Improves effectiveness, as opposed to efficiency, in the present position.

— Encourages objective analysis of qualifications and relationships.

— Relates progress to performance — are we doing the right things and are we doing the right things right?

— Assists in preparation for added responsibility.

The route to success in management begins with meeting objectives but goes far beyond. Sooner or later, the process of self-appraisal must emerge as the pivotal key. Self-appraisal is basic to the individual's growth plan. We are reluctant to work toward effective self-appraisal systems because we are unwilling to start with ourselves. When we do face up to this responsibility, another truth becomes evident — as managers become more objective and realistic about evaluating their own progress and performance, they simultaneously become more objective and realistic about the progress and performance of subordinates.

> *"The job of a professional manager is not to like people. It is not to change people. It is to put their strengths to work. And whether one approves of people or the way they do their work, their performance is the only thing that counts."*
> Peter Drucker –
> *My Years with General Motors*

The Step-By-Step Procedure

Why take the time to review formally the performance of an individual?

1. To try to improve performance on the job now held.
2. To develop people — and let it be known this is a primary concern.
3. To provide continuity of understanding and agreement on priorities and objectives.
4. To provide a basis for coordinating organization, unit and individual objectives.
5. To provide necessary documentation for appropriate personnel actions.

These essential needs can be met by following these steps:

STEP I: Employee Self-Appraisal

Just prior to the scheduled time for an appraisal interview, each individual should prepare a summary evaluation. It should include:

1. Objectives agreed upon at the beginning of the year, each quarter, etc.
2. Results achieved for each objective.
3. Extenuating circumstances involved where objectives were not met.
4. Accomplishments beyond previously agreed-upon goals.
5. Areas for personal growth and improvement and preparation for future career development.

STEP II: Supervisor Tentative Evaluation

At about the same time, the supervisor should make an independent summary judgment about the past performance of the individual covering the same points. This should not stress personality traits, but should cover the above points (a...e), as in Step I, plus a summary judgment evaluating the overall contribution of the individual to the organization.

Employee Self-Appraisal

Supervisor Tentative Evaluation

One-On-One Interview

STEP III: One-On-One Interview

In the interview the supervisor compares notes with the individual about progress, performance and potential. These guidelines are important:

1. Plan the interview carefully.
2. Establish a friendly atmosphere.
3. Let the employee talk first and present the summary he or she has prepared. Encourage personal analysis of performance in order to determine how to build on strengths and cope with weaknesses.
4. If necessary, take the initiative to help employee with analysis.
5. Concentrate on the positive aspects of performance and offer constructive criticism that points the way to future development.
6. Keep the discussion on measurable results and prepare objectives for the next operational period.
7. Get a commitment about work to be done to satisfy personal development needs.
8. Be willing to modify your preliminary judgments about performance based on new information and insights.
9. Share all this with the individual. Be sure he or she understands your judgment, even if agreement is not 100%. Work toward a good "batting average" of agreement.

Follow-Up During Year

STEP IV: Follow-Up During Year

Establish and maintain a performance file on each individual during the course of the appraisal period. To assist in making a meaningful appraisal the next time around, maintain a file of pertinent information (memos, reports, revised objectives, unusual achievements, interviews, etc.), that occurs during this time period and would be useful in making a results-oriented performance appraisal.

Here are the steps recommended to help you concentrate on results in the appraisal interview. Use it as a checklist next time you appraise an employee and see how many steps you accomplish.

Results-Oriented Performance Appraisal Interview Checklist

☐ Establish a friendly atmosphere by selecting the right time and place for the interview. Be sure the interview will be free from interruptions.

☐ Plan the interview carefully, selecting two or three key points that you want to be sure you get across. Concentrate on these main points as your objectives.

☐ Let the employee talk first, discussing a self-prepared summary memo. Be alert to this presentation for clues that may help you inject into the discussion the two or three main points you wish to make.

☐ Concentrate on the positive aspects of an employee's performance and offer constructive criticism that points the way toward future development. Rehashing past errors and failures should be done only to illustrate possible development needs. Remember, people tend to hear only the negative.

☐ Encourage the employee to analyze and appraise personal performance in order to determine areas of weakness and understand "why" the performance turned out the way it did. For example, this can be done by asking questions like: "What do you believe may have caused that project to fail?" or "Why do you suppose you feel this way?"

☐ At other times you may have to take the initiative and, as coach and counselor, point out to the employee why the performance failed or succeeded, what the employee's strengths and weaknesses are and how improvement might be made in the future.

☐ Make certain the discussion stays on specifics.

☐ Don't get bogged down in disagreement or arguments.

☐ Don't try to avoid the year's failure or lack of accomplishment. Listen to the employee's views and recognize the lack of achievement, but remember that last year is history. The discussion should center on what was learned from it, rather than justifying why it happened.

☐ Perhaps the cardinal rule is to remember you are the subordinate's manager: You are management. Therefore —

Never say "they" or, "I told them how you felt but they disagreed."

Say, "We discussed how you feel about this and reached the conclusion that..."

Self-Appraisal Inventory

If you have ever received or given an appraisal that was filled with controversy, you know the problems created. The inventory you are about to prepare is designed to make this a positive, developmental experience.

Managers should take two or three hours to answer the following questions before their next appraisal interview. Take time to think carefully about each question in sequence. You are encouraged to prepare preliminary drafts before the final version to be discussed with your supervisor.

What were my major achievements (results) in the past year and how were they related to my accountabilities (objectives)?

"We are made stronger on the realization that the helping band we need is at the end of our own right arm."
Sidney Phillips

166

Self-Appraisal Inventory 1

Accountabilities

In priority order, what did my boss and I agree that I was supposed to get done?

Measurements Used

Quantity, Quality, Time, Cost
(#, $, %, +, -)

Achievements

How did I do in meeting my objectives?

1. _____   _____   _____
   _____   _____   _____
   _____   _____   _____
   _____   _____   _____

2. _____   _____   _____
   _____   _____   _____
   _____   _____   _____
   _____   _____   _____

3. _____   _____   _____
   _____   _____   _____
   _____   _____   _____
   _____   _____   _____

4. _____   _____   _____
   _____   _____   _____
   _____   _____   _____
   _____   _____   _____

5. _____   _____   _____
   _____   _____   _____
   _____   _____   _____
   _____   _____   _____

6. _____   _____   _____
   _____   _____   _____
   _____   _____   _____
   _____   _____   _____

Self-Appraisal Inventory 2

What major dissatisfactions do
I have with my performance
during the past year?

Does my present boss agree?

1. _____
   _____
   _____

1. Yes___No___Reason(s):_____
   _____
   _____

2. _____
   _____
   _____

2. Yes___No___Reason(s):_____
   _____
   _____

3. _____
   _____
   _____

3. Yes___No___Reason(s):_____
   _____
   _____

What are my most important
assets in performing the job
I now hold?

Does my present boss agree?

1. _____
   _____
   _____

1. Yes___No___Reason(s):_____
   _____
   _____

2. _____
   _____
   _____

2. Yes___No___Reason(s):_____
   _____
   _____

3. _____
   _____
   _____

3. Yes___No___Reason(s):_____
   _____
   _____

On a scale of 1 – 100, how would I rate my chances of being selected for my present job if I
had to reapply in open competition?

_____

Why? _____

_____

Would I want to reapply?_____

If not, why not?_____

_____

Self-Appraisal Inventory 3

What can my immediate
supervisor do to help me do
a better job?

1. _____
_____
_____

2. _____
_____
_____

3. _____
_____
_____

Does my present boss agree?

1. Yes___No___Reason(s):_____
_____
_____

2. Yes___No___Reason(s):_____
_____
_____

3. Yes___No___Reason(s):_____
_____
_____

What would I most like to see
changed about the way our
department is run?

Need:_____
_____
_____

Yes___No___Reason(s):_____
_____
_____

Change Recommended:

1. _____
_____
_____
_____

2. _____
_____
_____
_____

3. _____
_____
_____
_____

Method to Accomplish:

1. _____
_____
_____
_____

2. _____
_____
_____
_____

3. _____
_____
_____
_____

Self-Study Questions for Supervisors

The self-study questions that follow have been designed to help you prepare a personal development plan. There are a total of five sections, each containing ten questions on how effective you or your subordinates are in that particular area. Score each question on the blanks provided. Total your score for the page at the bottom of the page.

If your score is 60 or less on any section, this is an area for which you should prepare a personal development plan. Mark the score for each section on the chart on page 153.

Definite Strength 10-9	Moderately Effective 8-7	Average Performance 6-5	Rarely Effective 4-3	Definite Weakness 2-1

I. Style

1. Am I sensitive to the influence my actions have on my subordinates?
   Comment: _____

2. Do I understand subordinates' reactions to my actions?
   Comment: _____

3. Do I find an appropriate balance between encouragement and pressure?
   Comment: _____

4. Do I allow subordinates to express ideas and opinions?
   Comment: _____

5. Am I effective at motivating subordinates?
   Comment: _____

6. Am I able to resolve conflicts in a constructive way?
   Comment: _____

7. Have I developed team spirit among my subordinates?
   Comment: _____

8. Do I have a clear understanding of my role in the organization?
   Comment: _____

9. Am I tactful in disciplining subordinates?
   Comment: _____

10. Do I have a personal plan for self-improvement?
    Comment: _____

Page Total: _____

Definite Strength 10-9	Moderately Effective 8-7	Average Performance 6-5	Rarely Effective 4-3	Definite Weakness 2-1

II. Planning

1. Are the operations of my organization balanced so that the pace of change is neither too routine nor too disruptive?
   Comment: _____

2. Do I sufficiently analyze the impact of particular changes on the future of our organization?
   Comment: _____

3. Am I sufficiently well informed to pass judgment on the proposals that my subordinates make?
   Comment: _____

4. Do I schedule my meetings appropriately?
   Comment: _____

5. Are my meetings well planned?
   Comment: _____

6. Do I have a clear vision of direction for my organization?
   Comment: _____

7. Are these plans in written form to guide myself as well as others?
   Comment: _____

8. Do I make them explicit in order to guide the decisions of others in the organization better?
   Comment: _____

9. Are they flexible enough to be changed, if necessary, to meet the changing needs of the organization?
   Comment: _____

10. Does the day-to-day work in my unit run smoothly?
    Comment: _____

Page Total: _____

> *"He who knows others is clever; he who knows himself is enlightened."*
> Lao Tse

Definite	Moderately	Average	Rarely	Definite
Strength	Effective	Performance	Effective	Weakness
10-9	8-7	6-5	4-3	2-1

III. Information — Communication

1. Do I have good sources of information and methods for obtaining it?
   Comment: _____

2. Is my information organized so that it is easy to locate and use?
   Comment: _____

3. Do I have other people do some of my research for me?
   Comment: _____

4. Do I make good use of my contacts to get information?
   Comment: _____

5. Do I balance information-collecting with action-taking? (Do I have what I need when I need it?)
   Comment: _____

6. Do my people have the information they need when they need it?
   Comment: _____

7. Do I "put it in writing" so that my subordinates are not at an informational disadvantage?
   Comment: _____

8. Do I use the different media appropriately? (Phone, memos, meetings, etc.)
   Comment: _____

9. Do I make the most of meetings for which I am responsible?
   Comment: _____

10. Do I spend enough time touring my organization to observe results accomplished first-hand?
    Comment: _____

Page Total: _____

Definite Strength 10-9	Moderately Effective 8-7	Average Performance 6-5	Rarely Effective 4-3	Definite Weakness 2-1

IV. Time Management

1. Do I have a time-scheduling system?
   Comment: _____

2. Do I avoid reacting to the pressures of the moment?
   Comment: _____

3. Do I avoid concentrating on one particular function
   or one type of problem just because I find it interesting?
   Comment: _____

4. Do I schedule particular kinds of work at special
   times of the day or week to take advantage of my
   own energy/effectiveness levels?
   Comment: _____

5. Am I in control of the amount of fragmentation and
   interruption of my work?
   Comment: _____

6. Do I balance current, tangible activities with time
   for reflection and planning?
   Comment: _____

7. Do key problems/priorities receive the attention
   they deserve?
   Comment: _____

8. Do I make use of time-saving devices, such as
   dictating machines and computers, when appropriate?
   Comment: _____

9. Do I have my priorities clearly in mind most of the time?
   Comment: _____

10. Do I have the necessary information available to me
    at the right time to meet my deadlines?
    Comment: _____

Page Total: _____

Definite Strength 10-9	Moderately Effective 8-7	Average Performance 6-5	Rarely Effective 4-3	Definite Weakness 2-1

V. Delegation

1. Do my subordinates understand our objectives and know what is to be done, when, how well and by whom?
Comment: _____

2. Do I know which of my responsibilities I must meet myself and which I can delegate?
Comment: _____

3. Do I encourage initiative in my subordinates?
Comment: _____

4. Do I leave the final decision to subordinates often enough?
Comment: _____

5. Do I avoid doing the work of my subordinates?
Comment: _____

6. Do I show genuine interest in the work my subordinates are doing?
Comment: _____

7. Am I confident that my subordinates can handle the work I give them?
Comment: _____

8. Do I give subordinates the guidance, training and authority they need to make decisions independently?
Comment: _____

9. Do I regularly assess the quality of my work and that of my subordinates?
Comment: _____

10. Do I use delegation to help my subordinates gain new skills and grow in the organization?
Comment: _____

Page Total: _____

Supervisory Self-Study Analysis — Composite Scores

Indicate your score for each section on the chart below and then draw a line connecting all scores (see example below). Add totals at the bottom of each column and divide grand total by 5 to get your Composite Score.

(Example)

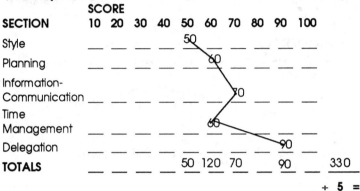

SECTION	SCORE 10	20	30	40	50	60	70	80	90	100
Style					50					
Planning						60				
Information-Communication							70			
Time Management					66					
Delegation									90	
TOTALS					50	120	70		90	330

÷ **5** =

Composite Score 66

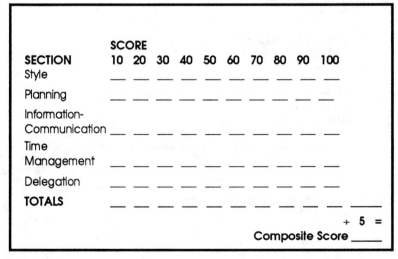

SECTION	SCORE 10	20	30	40	50	60	70	80	90	100
Style										
Planning										
Information-Communication										
Time Management										
Delegation										
TOTALS										

÷ **5** =

Composite Score _____

Score Range	Means:
80-100	Strong area — build on it!
60- 80	Acceptable but could be improved.
40- 60	Weak area — face up to it!
Under 40	Expect trouble if not improved soon.

Subordinate Skills Profile

Next, rate your individual subordinates on the statements below on a scale of 1-10 as indicated. Total the score for each section and mark it on the chart at the end of the evaluation (pg. 162).

Manager _____

Evaluator _____

Date _____

Definite Strength	Average	Definite Weakness
10-8	7-5	4-1

I. Planning

1. Understands job responsibilities and authority clearly.
   Comments: _____

2. Is able to formulate realistic plans and schedules.
   Comments: _____

3. Classifies the work to be done, divides it into components and creates orderly and productive arrangements.
   Comments: _____

4. Is able to utilize resources (manpower and other) productively.
   Comments: _____

5. Establishes priorities for work to be done, personally and by others.
   Comments: _____

6. Sees to it that each person understands his or her responsibility and authority.
   Comments: _____

7. Plans and conducts effective meetings as required and avoids unnecessary ones.
   Comments: _____

8. Uses meetings to develop people.
   Comments: _____

9. Shows people how each job fits into the total picture.
   Comments: _____

10. Makes sure that people have the equipment and materials they need to do their job.
    Comments: _____

Section Total: _____

Definite Strength
10-8

Average
7-5

Definite Weakness
4-1

II. Initiating

1. Recognizes and corrects situations that need improvement.
   Comments: _____

2. Is able to originate new approaches to problems.
   Comments: _____

3. Makes the most of a promising new plan or idea.
   Comments: _____

4. Puts worthwhile suggestions into operation.
   Comments: _____

5. Encourages subordinates to try new methods and new ideas.
   Comments: _____

6. Faces up to problems.
   Comments: _____

7. Begins on new projects without waiting to be told.
   Comments: _____

8. Seeks solutions rather than excuses.
   Comments: _____

9. Doesn't hesitate to ask questions to get needed information.
   Comments: _____

10. Is willing to take reasonable risks.
    Comments: _____

Section Total: _____

Definite Strength
10-8

Average
7-5

Definite Weakness
4-1

III. Delegating

1. Is able to effectively delegate responsibility and authority at all levels.
   Comments: _____

2. Avoids trespassing on authority, once delegated.
   Comments: _____

3. Periodically checks the performance of others on duties that have been delegated.
   Comments: _____

4. Is concerned with a minimum of detail.
   Comments: _____

5. Tries to define jobs delegated to others so as to provide them with the greatest challenge and opportunity.
   Comments: _____

6. Inspires in people the willingness to work toward objectives.
   Comments: _____

7. Makes full use of the skills and abilities of subordinates.
   Comments: _____

8. Provides know-how for subordinates as required.
   Comments: _____

9. Has subordinates participate in setting work objectives and schedules.
   Comments: _____

10. Tries to get group reaction on important matters before going ahead.
    Comments: _____

Section Total: _____

Definite Strength
10-8

Average
7-5

Definite Weakness
4-1

IV. Decision-Making

1. Decisions are consistent with policies, procedures
   and objectives of the organization.
   Comments: _____

2. Decisions are consistent with the economic, social
   and political climate.
   Comments: _____

3. Keeps within the bounds of authority and ability
   in making decisions.
   Comments: _____

4. Considers and correctly interprets key facts in
   solving problems.
   Comments: _____

5. Uses own experience and that of others in reaching
   conclusions.
   Comments: _____

6. Accepts responsibility for decisions, even when
   others are consulted.
   Comments: _____

7. Makes decisions promptly, but not hastily.
   Comments: _____

8. Makes decisions that are realistic and clear-cut.
   Comments: _____

9. Takes calculated risks, based on sound
   decision-making.
   Comments: _____

10. Converts decisions into effective and
    decisive action.
    Comments: _____

                            Section Total: _____

Definite Strength	Average	Definite Weakness
10-8	7-5	4-1

V. Communicating

1. Keeps informed on how subordinates are thinking and feeling.
Comments:

_____

2. Encourages others to express their ideas and opinions.
Comments:

_____

3. Listens with understanding and purpose.
Comments:

_____

4. Responds intelligently to criticisms of own actions.
Comments:

_____

5. Handles questions promptly.
Comments:

_____

6. Keeps people informed on changes, policies and procedures affecting their work.
Comments:

_____

7. Recognizes the good work of others and expresses appreciation.
Comments:

_____

8. Explains the "why" of decisions.
Comments:

_____

9. Makes significant contributions in meetings, both listening and speaking.
Comments:

_____

10. Expresses self clearly and effectively in writing and speaking.
Comments:

_____

Section Total: _____

Definite Strength	Average	Definite Weakness
10-8	7-5	4-1

IV. Developing

1. Selects properly qualified people for jobs.
   Comments: _____

2. Helps new employees adjust to the job and
   the group.
   Comments: _____

3. Creates in people a desire to do a better job.
   Comments: _____

4. Systematically evaluates the performance of
   each employee.
   Comments: _____

5. Keeps people informed on how they are doing.
   Comments: _____

6. Uses constructive criticism reflecting a helpful
   attitude.
   Comments: _____

7. Discusses career opportunities with subordinates.
   Comments: _____

8. Helps subordinates formulate self-improvement
   plans.
   Comments: _____

9. Informs higher authorities of subordinates'
   accomplishments and developments.
   Comments: _____

10. Has a plan for self-development and is actively
    engaged in it.
    Comments: _____

Section Total: _____

Definite Strength
10-8

Average
7-5

Definite Weakness
4-1

VII. Relationships

1. Is firm and fair in dealing with subordinates and associates.
Comments: _____

2. Is able to "take it" when the going is rough.
Comments: _____

3. Is able to show enjoyment of work and associates.
Comments: _____

4. Makes it easy for people to talk.
Comments: _____

5. Visits subordinates and associates in their offices and workplaces.
Comments: _____

6. Is interested in the personal well-being of others.
Comments: _____

7. Understands how off-the-job problems can be related to on-the-job performance.
Comments: _____

8. Participates appropriately in community activities.
Comments: _____

9. Tactfully adjusts to personalities and circumstances.
Comments: _____

10. Sells ideas to others without pressure.
Comments: _____

Section Total: _____

Definite Strength	Average	Definite Weakness
10-8	7-5	4-1

VIII. Standards

1. Uses systematic methods to measure performance, productivity, and progress.
   Comments: _____

2. Jointly develops objectives and performance standards with subordinates.
   Comments: _____

3. Evaluates continually to readjust the organization and work standards.
   Comments: _____

4. Sees that standard operating practices are followed when necessary.
   Comments: _____

5. Fixed accountability.
   Comments: _____

6. Faces up to failures in meeting standards.
   Comments: _____

7. Does not seek goals that are unreasonably high.
   Comments: _____

8. Does not settle for goals that are too easily accomplished.
   Comments: _____

9. Is willing to negotiate range of performance when a precise standard is not necessary.
   Comments: _____

Section Total: _____

183

Subordinate Skills Profile — Composite Scores

Individual Skill Score Range Means:

80-100	Strong area — Subordinate should build on it!
60- 80	Acceptable but could be improved.
40- 60	Weak area — Subordinate should face up to it!
Under 40	Expect trouble if not improved soon.

Composite Scoring

Indicate your employee's score for each section of the skills assessment on the chart below and draw a line connecting all scores (see example on next page). Use variations to determine where improvement effort should be concentrated. Add totals at bottom of each column and divide grand total by 8 to get **Composite Score.**

SKILL	SCORE 10 20 30 40 50 60 70 80 90 100
Planning	— — — — — — — — — —
Initiating	— — — — — — — — — —
Delegating	— — — — — — — — — —
Decision-Making	— — — — — — — — — —
Communicating	— — — — — — — — — —
Developing	— — — — — — — — — —
Relationships	— — — — — — — — — —
Standards	— — — — — — — — — —
TOTALS	— — — — — — — — — — ___

+ 8 =

Composite Score _____

If Composite Score Is:

80-100	Strengths should serve subordinate well if exploited.
60- 80	Unbalanced skills may retard subordinate's progress.
Under 50	Subordinate may be mismatched as a supervisor.

184

(Example)

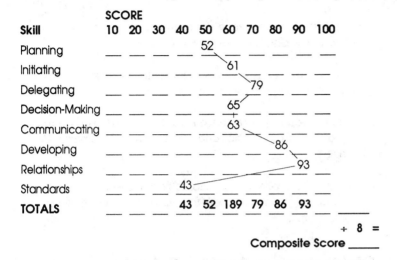

Skill	SCORE									
	10	20	30	40	50	60	70	80	90	100
Planning					52					
Initiating						61				
Delegating							79			
Decision-Making						65				
Communicating						63				
Developing								86		
Relationships									93	
Standards				43						
TOTALS				43	52	189	79	86	93	

÷ 8 =

Composite Score _____

When you have rated subordinates and have marked the final
score for each section on the chart on the previous page, ask
subordinates to rate themselves and compare your composite
score chart with theirs. Check to see where you agree and
disagree. Discuss how you will maintain the areas of strength
(above 80%) that you agreed upon. Discuss what specifically will
be done to correct the areas of weakness (below 50%) agreed
upon.

Now that we have reviewed the basics of self-appraisal and
the two detailed profiling methods, let's look at how to assure
that we are concentrating on RESULTS in the appraisal
process. This is essential unless we are willing to allow other
factors like seniority, "experience," credentials, social ties or
personality factors to prevail.

Description of Results-Oriented Performance Appraisal

1. It is a system of evaluating performance based on success or failure in meeting predetermined objectives.

2. It requires managers and subordinates to establish performance objectives jointly.

3. An evaluation of performance is made by both manager and employee with the advice and concurrence of the next level manager.

4. It stresses the importance of a face-to-face discussion between manager and subordinate, both for setting objectives and for evaluating performance.

Objectives of Results-Oriented Performance Appraisal

1. Improve present performance.

2. Develop people for added responsibility.

3. Answer employees' two most basic questions:
   a. How am I doing?
   b. Where do I go from here?

4. Provide coordination of departmental and individual goals.

5. Determine personnel actions (salary, promotion, transfer, etc.).

The Case of the Performance Gap

"Look, George," Lew Young said. "I thought we understood each other, but apparently I was wrong. Don't you remember our conversation last year at this time?"

"My 'appraisal' interview? Sure, I remember," George Fisk answered. "But you're saying a lot of things now that you didn't tell me then."

This was George's second year in Lew's department, and although Lew considered him capable and talented, he thought that George was spending too much time in the office and not enough outside looking for new business. Both parts of the job were important, but George seemed much happier in the office than out in the field.

During that talk a year ago, when Lew and George had talked about George's performance, Lew thought he had made it clear that he expected George to spend more time outside the office with the salesmen who reported to him, building up the company's business. But George didn't seem to get the message.

"Last year, George," Lew said, "I said that you should spend less time at your desk and more time outside in the field drumming up business. But if anything, your outside activities have been less frequent during the past year. I'm afraid that isn't very satisfactory."

"Wait a minute," George said. "You told me that we needed more business, but you didn't tell me to spend more time outside. At least, I didn't understand it that way."

"George," Lew said, "I made that point because that's the weakest part of your performance, and I wanted to see it improve during the year. I thought that was understood."

"Well, it wasn't," George said. "I got the impression that I was doing pretty well, and now you spring this on me."

**C
A
S
E

S
T
U
D
Y**

Comment

Why did this gap in performance expectation develop? It's probably a combination of factors. For one thing, Lew must have spoken in generalities during the first interview, so the message he was trying to get across to George didn't get through.

Moreover, from past performance, Lew should have realized that George preferred inside work to going out in the field. Knowing that he felt that way, Lew should have spent more time during the initial interview to get some feedback to ensure that George was understanding the importance of what he wanted.

In other words, Lew failed to be precise, to consider the "whats" (new business expected) vs. the "hows" (more time outside the office), and to get the feedback he needed to be certain that he and George understood each other. Finally, he should have put it in writing in terms of measurable goals and results.

This case illustrates the vital importance of both parties listening and learning from the performance appraisal interview. By avoiding these common sources of error, the appraisal process can be one of the most valuable developmental experiences you can have.

"Use the talents you possess; for the woods would be very silent if no birds sang except the best."

Sources of Error in Appraisals

Below are eight sources that could lead to misunderstanding
between an employee and his or her supervisor. Explain why it is
important to avoid these sources of error in the performance
appraisal process.

1. Unwillingness to take time and effort to do the appraisal
   thoroughly.
   Why avoid?

2. Favoring certain people over others regardless of
   performance.
   Why avoid?

3. Overweighting of recent occurrences.
   Why avoid?

4. Personal prejudices or bias on the part of the rater.
   Why avoid?

5. Lack of uniform criteria or job standards.
   Why avoid?

6. Reluctance to point out weaknesses.
   Why avoid?

7. Appraisal forms more concerned with personality traits than
   with objectives.
   Why avoid?

8. "Pleasing the boss" earns higher rating than job effectiveness.
   Why avoid?

Which of these errors was Lew guilty of?

Which are problems for you? For your boss?

When properly understood and prepared, the appraisal process should not be dreaded or feared by either the appraiser or the subordinate. The appraisal does not "stand alone." It is, in a sense, the culmination or peak of an effective Performance-Based Management System. Tying appraisals to objectives is the key. This can be done by establishing and maintaining a formal goal-setting system and a vigorous appraisal process.

Performance Improvement Principles

To gain maximum benefit from appraisals, it is helpful to think in terms of the basic principles we believe to be involved in determining what performance can be. Here is my list:

Ten Principles to Improve Performance

1. In any decision-making process, those who will be affected by the decision should be informed and, when appropriate, consulted.

2. The goals of the organization should be clearly understood by those who will do the work.

3. The goals of individuals should be negotiated in terms of consistency with the goals of the organization.

4. When responsibility is delegated, as it should and must be in any organization, corresponding authority should be delegated within reasonable limits.

5. As a general rule, the responsible person nearest to the involved situation should make the decision.

6. Consistent effort should be made to enable all in the organization to understand the principle that there must be a relationship between responsibility and competence.

7. The practice of basic courtesy is essential in building goodwill.

8. The people who are consulted when a decision is being made should be helped to understand the way in which their advice or counsel will be used.

9. Favoritism, or what appears to be favoritism, is especially harmful to morale.

10. In dealing with problems, seek solutions, not blame.

When all is said and done, your success as a manager depends on how effective you and your subordinates are in working together as a team. In most organizations, how effective we are means how productive we are. And, in most situations, productivity can be measured as a high-priority desired result. The challenge then is to make yourself productive!

Qualities of High-Productivity Managers

Here is what studies at the University of Michigan over a 25-year period have shown.

High-Productivity Managers:

— Place less direct emphasis on production as a goal.

— Are more employee-centered.

— Are good communicators who keep employees informed.

— Encourage employee participation in making decisions.

— Spend more time in supervising and less time in doing production work.

— Are less closely supervised by their own supervisors.

— Have a greater feeling of confidence in their supervisory role.

— Feel they know where they stand within the organization.

Question: Does your experience indicate that other qualities should be listed?

> *Every time The Tonight Show theme is played, Paul Anka (who wrote the theme in 1962) collects $200.*

Other factors, beyond productivity, are also important. They all involve experience and a willingness to be both introspective and objective in analyzing personal needs and progress.

Keys to Managerial Success

Have a team concept. Managers should care about the organization's progress and the people who work with them and for them, and should show it.

Work on your weak points. Take a good look at yourself and be sure you're completely honest when you do so. A person who is honest can pretty well sum up his or her strengths and weaknesses on the job.

Learn how to delegate skillfully. Perhaps one of the biggest hurdles for a manager is learning how to let go of an old job. Being willing to delegate is not enough in itself. It must be done with thought and skill. Over-delegation can be as harmful as under-delegation.

Be realistic about inadequate subordinates. A manager should not let incompetent people drag him or her down. Once you lose confidence in a person and your efforts to help him or her improve have failed, you must have the courage to face up to a change.

Concentrate on preparation. Good preparation breeds confidence. Combining preparation with enthusiasm is the way to put your ideas across successfully.

Develop confidence. Nobody is born with confidence. It has to be developed — the hard way. Confidence starts with successful accomplishment, and you can build on it day by day.

Don't think in black and white. Make certain that you examine the other person's viewpoint fairly. Flexibility is an important requirement for successful management.

Look to the future. Don't be satisfied with past successes. Each new job has its own standards for accomplishment.

Know where your time goes. Take care to concentrate on your most important responsibilities and schedule your efforts accordingly.

Questions for Personal Development

1. What is the major emphasis of this chapter?

2. What do you feel are the most important things you learned from this chapter?
   1)

   2)

   3)

3. How can you apply what you learned to your current job?
   1)

   2)

   3)

4. What objectives will you set to improve? By when (date)?
   1)

   2)

   3)

5. Who can help you most in applying what you learned in this chapter?

6. What are the major roadblocks you expect that may hinder your progress in applying what you learned in this chapter?

   Roadblock   **Why?**
   1)
   2)
   3)

7. How will you communicate the most important points in this chapter to your key people?

8. What preparation is necessary for this introduction?

9. What changes do you expect to make that will achieve greater motivation of your team?

Change   **By when (date)?**

1)

2)

3)

10. How will you monitor to assure that performance has improved, i.e., productivity has increased? (Reports, meetings, etc.)

11. What work-related problems concern you most in evaluating how you will benefit from this chapter?

12. Once you've accomplished several milestones, how will you continue developing new ideas and objectives related to this chapter?

13. How would you summarize the change you expect to see in yourself one year from now as a result of what you learned in this chapter?

Motivation and Teamwork

Organizations depend on individuals who have learned how to work together effectively. Therefore, development of individuals is essential for the improvement of every organization. Increasing skills is vital to the development of managers and those who work with them. We need help to reach our goals. Developing the talents of your people not only helps you obtain your goals, but is also one of the greatest joys of working. In addition to their paychecks, people are entitled to grow in return for their investment of time and talent.

Motivation, delegation, time management and communication skills are "enablers" that help people perform more efficiently and effectively. The confidence that follows an increased sense of accomplishment sparks new incentive and drive.

You will evaluate your skills in each of these areas in the following chapters. With every exercise, it is very important that you relate the questions to your own job. As you complete each chapter, fill out the appropriate forms to summarize key topics and provide a concise action plan so you can focus your efforts.

"You can preach a better sermon with your life than with your lips."
Goldsmith

In building an effective management team we must not only consider our own leadership style, we must evaluate the behavior patterns of others as well. The objective is to utilize talents and experiences that will supplement and complement each other. Before we can make these assessments, we need to become familiar with several basic types of behaviors. Study these four behavior patterns in terms of motivation and answer the questions that follow.

Managerial Behavior Skills...

Support-Giving

Trusting. Responsive. Idealistic. Tries to do his or her best in assigned tasks. Sets high standards for self and staff. Highly receptive to ideas of others. Cooperates readily. Helpful. A natural team player.

Problems

Trust can become gullibility. Desire for excellence can extend to impracticality.

Motivation Keys

Stress worthwhile causes. Appeal to idealism and a sense of excellence. Ask for help. Show personal concern for progress. Emphasize personal development goals. Be accessible — give trust and recognition.

Control-Thinking

Openly aggressive. A go-getter. Acts quickly. Expresses self-confidence. Persuasive — very competitive. Takes charge and wants little, if any, supervision. Tells you what needs to be done.

Problems

Initiative can become impulsiveness. Confidence can become arrogance.

Motivation Keys

Appeal to competitive drive. Give maximum responsibility and authority. Avoid looking over his or her shoulder. Provide resources to achieve goals. Set boundaries, but appreciate initiative.

Conserving — Holding

Methodical and precise. Analyzes alternatives thoroughly. Practical — makes the most of existing resources. Often reserved and unenthusiastic. Does a predictable, efficient job.

Problems

Careful can become nitpicking. Methodical can become plodding. Analytical can become "analysis paralysis."

Motivation Keys

Aim at methodical nature. Present ideas as low risk. In launching new projects, accent links to existing areas. Show you are objective, fair and consistent. Set out details clearly — be well organized. Systematically review how things are going.

Adapting — Dealing

Flexible. Enthusiastic. Tactful. Never seems to make enemies. Sensitive to what others want and modifies own approach accordingly. Seeks popularity and the spotlight. Open to new ideas. Excites co-workers and subordinates to do the job at hand.

Problems

Flexibility becomes inconsistency. Tactfulness becomes too agreeable.

Motivation Keys

Capitalize on the project's social elements. Be informative — give him or her helpful feedback. Keep the relationship friendly and relaxed. Keep manager's role central.

"I was so ambitious I didn't even know I was ambitious. I believed so thoroughly that I was going to be a star... I never felt that humiliation, that rebuff, or I would have freaked out completely."
Richard Dreyfuss

Management Style Worksheet

Management Style

1. Which of these is your style most of the time or under normal circumstances?

    _____ Support-Giving

    _____ Control-Taking

    _____ Conserving/Holding

    _____ Adapting/Dealing

2. Why do you believe this is so?

3. Which is your boss's prevailing style?

    _____ Support-Giving

    _____ Control-Taking

    _____ Conserving/Holding

    _____ Adapting/Dealing

4. Why do you believe this is so? Recent examples?

5. Action you plan to take to develop a better team relationship with your boss:

6. What will you do?

7. When will you do it?

Now consider each of the people who report directly to you. What is their prevailing style?

Subordinate Style Worksheet

_____   _____
          Name   Prevailing style

Recent evidence, examples, illustrations of behavior that lead you to this conclusion:

Action you plan to take to help this person develop a better team relationship with you:

What will you do?

When will you do it?

Complete this worksheet for each of your subordinates.

199

It's no secret that those people who are highly motivated will accomplish the most. They bring their own motivation to work. They don't need to be prodded or pushed. With each task completed, they have a feeling of satisfaction that provides incentive to accomplish even more, and so on. The process becomes a productive "Catch 22" — how can I outdo myself?

How do we get this increased sense of accomplishment in our situation? There is a close relationship between ...

Competence and Performance

Competent people achieve goals. Competence grows when people:

1. Know what is expected of them.
2. Know what they expect of themselves.
3. Know their own limitations.
4. Know where to get help.
5. Can work without direction.
6. Constantly measure their own performance against their own goals.
7. Are comfortable with the idea that rewards will follow achievement.

> *"If you can't convince them, confuse them."*
> Harry Truman

200

WORKSHEET RATINGS

Now rate each of your subordinates from 1-5 on the
Competence and Performance Scale.

1 = lowest ranking

2 = below par

3 = par/satisfactory

4 = above par

5 = highest ranking

Subordinate names:

A is _____

B is _____

C is _____

D is _____

| | Rating (1-5) | | | |
	A	B	C	D
1. Knows what is expected.	____	____	____	____
2. Knows what he or she expects of himself or herself.	____	____	____	____
3. Knows own limitations.	____	____	____	____
4. Knows where to get help.	____	____	____	____
5. Can work without direction.	____	____	____	____
6. Constantly measures own performance against goals.	____	____	____	____
7. Comfortable with idea that rewards follow achievement.	____	____	____	____

"An honest executive is one who shares the credit with the person who did all the work."

Basic Motivation Requirements

In order to achieve the optimum conditions for motivating employees to perform at their highest level, there needs to be...

1. Supervisors Who:

— are approachable and open-minded.

— share information before it's needed.

— encourage initiative.

— help people learn from mistakes.

— give credit when due.

2. A Process for Setting Goals That:

— relates organizational goals to personal goals.

— helps people set goals and measure their own progress.

— stresses negotiation of results expected in advance.

3. A Management System That:

— enables individuals to achieve personal goals by achieving organizational goals.

— can be managed by people rather than stifling them.

— reveals a developmental (vs. authoritarian) approach to supervision.

Which of these requirements are met in your organization?

Which are not being met?

Which requirements are not being met in your unit?

What steps can you take to improve the situation?

> *"To err is human, to forgive is not company policy."*

De-Motivate or Activate?

Are you guilty of de-motivating your employees? Are you aware of what things activate your employees? Evaluate your performance in the following exercise.

People are "de-motivated" when you:

Avoiding these de-motivators?

	My Self-Rating			
Poor	Average		Excellent	
1	2	3	4	5

1. Fail to give them your undivided attention. — — — — —
2. Fail to acknowledge their personal preferences. — — — — —
3. Belittle their accomplishments. — — — — —
4. Criticize them in front of others. — — — — —
5. Are insensitive to time schedules. — — — — —
6. Waiver in making a decision. — — — — —
7. Do not complete your part of the work. — — — — —
8. Are preoccupied with your own projects. — — — — —
9. Show favoritism. — — — — —
10. Delay discussing their concerns. — — — — —

People are "activated" when you:

Using these activators ?

	My Self-Rating			
Poor	Average		Excellent	
1	2	3	4	5

1. Challenge them with important work. — — — — —
2. Provide necessary support services. — — — — —
3. Let them know what is expected. — — — — —
4. Recognize their accomplishments appropriately. — — — — —
5. Keep them informed of changes that may affect them. — — — — —
6. Communicate progress regularly. — — — — —
7. Face up to needed personnel changes and assignments. — — — — —
8. Seek their advice sincerely. — — — — —
9. Demonstrate confidence in them. — — — — —
10. Encourage ingenuity. — — — — —

What Makes People Perform?

A few years ago, the United States Chamber of Commerce conducted a study involving 40,000 hourly employees and 5,000 of their supervisors. Employees were asked to rate their job conditions as described below, using a scale from 1 to 10. Their bosses were asked to rank the same items as they believed their employees would rank them.

Job conditions	Rating (from 1 to 10)
Full appreciation of work done.	_____
Feeling "in" on things.	_____
Sympathetic help on personal problems.	_____
Job security.	_____
Good wages.	_____
Work that keeps you interested.	_____
Promotion and growth in the company.	_____
Personal loyalty to workers.	_____
Good working conditions.	_____
Tactful discipline.	_____

How do you believe your employees would rank these ten items in your work environment? (1 being the most important to them and 10 being the least important.)

As a group, the 40,000 employees ranked these items in the following order, from most important to least important:

1. Job security.
2. Good wages.
3. Full appreciation of work done.
4. Feeling "in" on things.
5. Work that keeps you interested.
6. Good working conditions.
7. Promotion and growth in the company.
8. Tactful discipline.
9. Sympathetic help on personal problems.
10. Personal loyalty to workers.

The 5,000 supervisors, however, said that the workers would rank them in this order:

1. Good wages.
2. Job security.
3. Promotion and growth in the company.
4. Good working conditions.
5. Work that keeps you interested.
6. Personal loyalty to workers.
7. Tactful discipline.
8. Full appreciation of work done.
9. Sympathetic help on personal problems.
10. Feeling "in" on things.

Note the marked differences in viewpoint. The workers ranked appreciation third, for example, and promotion and growth seventh; their supervisors had the two completely reversed.

Similarly, the workers indicated that it's much more important to feel "in" on things than their supervisors thought. Conversely, the workers thought a lot less of "loyalty" than their bosses thought they would.

If your rankings differ significantly from those of the workers in this survey, it would be a good idea to re-examine how realistic your views are compared with those of non-supervisors.

> *"Success is all it's cracked up to be. Life gets better, the work is nicer and I'm nicer."*
> Daniel Travanti

There are other criteria for determining...

What Makes a Motivating Job?

Enrichment Characteristics:

Skill Variety: Doing different things; using different skills, abilities and talents.

Task Identity: Doing a job from beginning to end; the whole job rather than bits and pieces.

Task Significance: The degree of meaningful impact the job has; the importance of the job.

Autonomy: Freedom to do the work; discretion in scheduling, decision-making and means for accomplishing a job.

Feedback: Clear and direct information about job outcomes or performance.

Goal Characteristics:

Priority: Knowing and understanding what specific objectives or goals apply to the job and their relative priorities.

Difficulty: The amount of challenge inherent in the goal; the degree of uncertainty concerning goal accomplishment.

Determining the requirements for a motivating job is the first step to employee satisfaction. The next step involves building commitment.

Morale and Motivation Worksheet

Let's get more specific! What steps can you take to motivate employees and improve morale?

1. Consult employees in advance about contemplated changes to get their solutions and get them more involved. Use more group problem-solving.

This action applies
to my work with _____
                (Name of Employee)

I will take the following steps no later than_____.
                                  (final date)

Step 1_____ by_____.
                                             (date)

Step 2_____ by_____.
                                             (date)

Step 3 _____ by_____.
                                             (date)

2. Enlarge and diversify jobs, where practicable, to make them more challenging and interesting.

This action applies
to my work with _____
                (Name of Employee)

I will take the following steps no later than_____.
                                  (final date)

Step 1_____ by_____.
                                             (date)

Step 2_____ by_____.
                                             (date)

Step 3 _____ by_____.
                                             (date)

3. Keep employees better informed about what is going on in the organization.

This action applies
to my work with _____
                (Name of Employee)

I will take the following steps no later than_____.
                                       (final date)

Step 1_____ by_____.
                                                   (date)

Step 2_____ by_____.
                                                   (date)

Step 3 _____ by_____.
                                                   (date)

4. Do more and better coaching and counseling of employees and show greater interest in their development.

This action applies
to my work with _____
                (Name of Employee)

I will take the following steps no later than_____.
                                       (final date)

Step 1_____ by_____.
                                                   (date)

Step 2_____ by_____.
                                                   (date)

Step 3 _____ by_____.
                                                   (date)

5. Take time to explain why a job or procedure is necessary to gain greater understanding and acceptance of directions given.

This action applies
to my work with _____
                (Name of Employee)

I will take the following steps no later than_____.
                                       (final date)

Step 1_____ by_____.
                                                   (date)

Step 2_____ by_____.
                                                   (date)

Step 3 _____ by_____.
                                                   (date)

6. Give credit promptly and sincerely for a job well done.

This action applies
to my work with _____
(Name of Employee)

I will take the following steps no later than_____.
(final date)

Step 1_____ by_____.
(date)

Step 2_____ by_____.
(date)

Step 3 _____ by_____.
(date)

7. Criticize only privately and only job performance rather than the personal qualities of the employee.

This action applies
to my work with _____
(Name of Employee)

I will take the following steps no later than_____.
(final date)

Step 1_____ by_____.
(date)

Step 2_____ by_____.
(date)

Step 3 _____ by_____.
(date)

8. Invite suggestions for improvement from employees.

This action applies
to my work with _____
(Name of Employee)

I will take the following steps no later than_____.
(final date)

Step 1_____ by_____.
(date)

Step 2_____ by_____.
(date)

Step 3 _____ by_____.
(date)

9. Make greater effort to get more than superficially acquainted with employ-ees, thereby giving them more recognition.

This action applies
to my work with _____
                          (Name of Employee)

I will take the following steps no later than _____.
                                        (final date)

Step 1_____ by_____.
                                               (date)

Step 2_____ by_____.
                                               (date)

Step 3 _____ by_____.
                                               (date)

10. Improve listening skills and take more time to listen to employees.

This action applies
to my work with _____
                          (Name of Employee)

I will take the following steps no later than_____.
                                          (final date)

Step 1_____ by_____.
                                               (date)

Step 2_____ by_____.
                                             (date)

Step 3 _____ by_____.
                                               (date)

Let's look at a specific example of how one supervisor solved a problem in his unit and was able to motivate his entire team.

Pioneer National Bank

Bill Lehman was supervisor of the Electronic Data Processing Section at the Pioneer National Bank. He had been with the bank more than fifteen years.

When Lehman first joined Pioneer, all the work done by the Data Processing Section was done manually by 15 clerks. As the bank grew in size, and as new EDP equipment became available, the Data Processing Section expanded to its present level of 57 people.

Lehman needed a supervisor for the Key Punch Unit. His first choice was Paula MacCormack, who had been with the bank for six years.

Everyone recognized that Paula's work was outstanding. She was fast and accurate. However, while she produced more than anyone else, she preferred working alone.

This attitude sometimes created a problem. The Key Punch Unit had to meet frequent deadlines. Productivity depended on the close teamwork of the eight people involved.

Even when the entire group worked on the same project, Paula was reluctant to help out when her own part of the work was done. At times, she became upset if Lehman gave her extra work to meet the unit's deadlines.

This irritated the other people. As a result, the Key Punch Unit had less teamwork than Lehman would have liked. He had been meaning to talk to Paula and the others about this problem, but hadn't gotten around to it.

The lack of cooperation in the Key Punch Unit was one reason he wanted a competent person in charge, someone who could give full-time attention to improving the teamwork and output.

**C
A
S
E

S
T
U
D
Y**

211

CASE STUDY

Lehman analyzed the situation this way:

Paula was outstanding alone, but a poor performer as a member of the group. If she were promoted, could she build the team spirit the Key Punch Unit needed?

Lehman had several other alternatives.

He could leave the group without a leader and continue to supervise it himself. This had gotten to be quite time-consuming for him. Or he could promote one of the other people in the group who was less capable but a better team worker than Paula. That, of course, might cause other problems.

If you were Bill Lehman, what would you do?

What Actually Happened

Bill Lehman spent several weeks thinking about whether or not to promote Paula MacCormack. He decided he couldn't do it, despite her skills, until her team spirit improved. He also decided that perhaps he was partly to blame for the lack of cooperation in the Key Punch Unit. After all, he had never talked to Paula, or anyone else for that matter, about it.

To improve the team effort, Lehman set up a series of one-hour meetings each Friday, to review the coming week's schedule. When he brought up the subject of teamwork at the first meeting, people were at first reluctant to speak up. However, he encouraged everybody to talk freely and soon everyone, Paula included, was making suggestions on how cooperation might be improved.

Just recognizing the importance of teamwork improved operations in the Key Punch Unit almost immediately. In the following weeks, Paula's attitude (and team performance) gradually got better. After three months, productivity improved to the point that Lehman promoted Paula MacCormack. Her promotion was accepted by the other people and she turned out to be an excellent supervisor.

Analysis

Supervisor Bill Lehman's assessment regarding Paula MacCormack's potential as a unit leader was a good one. Even with her skills, she could not lead her unit successfully if she did not believe in or inspire a team spirit among her co-workers. His solution – creating a spirit of teamwork in Paula and the rest of the unit by involving them in a team effort – was an excellent one.

In Your Job...

1. In what specific ways is teamwork important to your group's success?

2. Are you treating your people as important, equal members of the team? ☐ Yes ☐ No

3. Does each of your people understand what the group as a whole is trying to accomplish? ☐ Yes ☐ No

4. Note below the last time you discussed teamwork with your people.

5. Which of your people tend to go their separate ways? Why? List their names with the reasons alongside each.

6. Note at least two things you might do to improve teamwork.

"Happiness is not the absence of conflict, but the ability to cope with it."

Bill Lehman's unit is well on its way to being a team. His choice of Paula as a team leader was sound. People working together as an effective team can accomplish far more than could the same number of individuals independently — so concentrate on these....

Six Ways to Improve Teamwork

Action	Checkpoint
1. Stress team goals; emphasize the common purpose.	Clarify and repeat goals often.
2. Let your people in on goals.	Be sure there is agreement.
3. Focus on cooperation.	Diagnose reasons for success in detail so everyone understands them.
4. Show your people how they can help one another.	Commend and highlight supportive work.
5. Emphasize the importance of each person's job to the group's success.	Demonstrate and dramatize the effects of failed assignments.
6. Treat each person as a valued member of your team, and he or she will more likely start being one.	Seek recommendations from <u>everyone</u>!

Summary:
How to Build Commitment

Ask yourself, "How committed am I to my own overall organizational objectives?" One thing is certain — subordinates can't provide your commitment. If you are satisfied with your level of commitment, then:

1. Weigh the commitment of your subordinates.

   — Is it sufficient?

   — Or is commitment obviously lacking?

2. Thoroughly discuss with subordinates the differences between your commitment and theirs.

   — What is the difference in commitment to overall organizational objectives? To departmental objectives? To personal job objectives?

3. Discuss possible action areas, inviting feedback. Agree upon commitment to specific action items.

   — Remember that commitments made in the presence of peers offer added motivation and communication as well.

4. Hold up your part of the agreement by providing the necessary communication, decisions and action.

   — Your actions are vital to your team.

5. Regularly discuss with subordinates the steps being taken and your role, as well as theirs, as a part of the ongoing learning process.

   — This is important whether or not the project is going well.

> *"There are two ways of being rich. One is to have all you want, the other is to be satisfied with all that you have."*

Questions for Personal Development

1. What is the major emphasis of this chapter?

2. What do you feel are the most important things you learned from this chapter?

    1)

    2)

    3)

3. How can you apply what you learned to your current job?

    1)

    2)

    3)

4. What objectives will you set to improve? By when (date)?

    1)

    2)

    3)

5. Who can help you most in applying what you learned in this chapter?

6. What are the major roadblocks you expect may hinder your progress in applying what you learned in this chapter?

    Roadblock   **Why?**

    1)

    2)

    3)

7. How will you communicate the most important points in this chapter to your key people?

8. What preparation is necessary for this introduction?

9. What changes do you expect to make that will achieve greater motivation of your team?

Change   **By when (date)?**

1)

2)

3)

10. How will you monitor to assure that performance has improved, i.e., productivity has increased? (Reports, meetings, etc.)

11. What work-related problems concern you most in evaluating how you will benefit from this chapter?

12. Once you've accomplished several milestones, how will you continue developing new ideas and objectives related to this chapter?

13. How would you summarize the change you expect to see in yourself one year from now as a result of what you learned in this chapter?

C HAPTER 9

Communication

Up to this point, we have discussed several keys to effective management. In this chapter, we will be reviewing an element of management that, in essence, brings all of the others together.

A common complaint among managers at any level has always been, "I wasn't aware of that" or "my boss never told me that." When true, progress is difficult and expectations may be unknown. Even if untrue, these comments set the stage for perfect alibis when goals are not met.

The solution is improved communication. When in doubt, revise, repeat and put it in writing. Hone your listening and questioning skills. This chapter will provide the tools that will enable you to improve as a communicator in some very practical ways.

Communication is the element that can make or break a relationship. Your progress as a manager can hinge on this vital ingredient even if you are generally effective in other areas of management. So let's consider the question:

Why Inform?

> "Of all the things you wear, your expression is the most important."

- Because information and access to information are primary sources of power.

  Lesson: If you want weak people – tell them little and keep lots of secrets!

- Because people are most likely to do what is expected if they know what is expected.

  Lesson: Explain, explain, explain.

- Because people can usually find ways to meet expectations and performance requirements if given feedback about results.

  Lesson: People are more likely to misinterpret what they don't know than what they do know – so tell them!

- Because productivity can be increased when job incumbents receive clear and concise information about performance requirements and results.

  Lesson: To withhold needed information is to retard productivity.

This case illustrates several reasons for keeping your staff informed. As you read it, put yourself in the place of the supervisor, Lloyd Johnson.

"If You Knew What I Know"

The Midwest Insurance Company, an old-line firm, employs several thousand people. In addition to life insurance, the company issues accident and health insurance, including group coverage. The company's home office, located in Illinois, handles the issuing of policies and maintaining of policy records. It is also responsible for accounting, agency supervision, claim settlement and a variety of other insurance services.

Company management had felt for some time that considerable amounts of money could be saved if some of the manual office procedures were computerized. It was decided to convert all the premium billing and record maintenance to business machine operation.

Lloyd Johnson, Supervisor of Accounting, was appointed to head a task force to plan and direct the changeover.

Johnson had been with the company a number of years. He was loyal, hard-working, very cautious and methodical. He decided it would be in the company's best interest to keep the whole thing secret until the change actually took place, in about six months. Not all of the committee members agreed with Johnson, but they went along at his insistence.

However, it was impossible to keep the information secret, and it soon leaked out. Rumors spread like wildfire, making everyone nervous — particularly newer employees. The committee learned, for example, that several people, fearing they might lose their jobs, had filed applications for employment with other insurance companies.

Because of the growing morale problem, an emergency meeting of the committee was called. Despite the problems being created, Johnson still felt that the release of any information might be misleading, since plans for how the conversion would be carried out were not yet final.

C A S E S T U D Y

A preliminary plan would be completed in about two months, and he wanted to wait at least until then before releasing anything. He reasoned that giving people premature and incomplete information would only raise more questions than could be answered, thus creating even greater uncertainty.

Johnson wanted to do what was best for the company but, in view of the problems that had come up, he was beginning to have doubts as to whether he was following the right course.

If you were supervisor Lloyd Johnson, what would you do?

What Actually Happened

At the committee meeting, John Magill, Supervisor of Records, said that several of his people had come to him greatly worried. He added that he had a tough time answering questions because of the committee agreement to "keep the matter secret."

The other committee members agreed that employees should be told what's going on, and finally convinced Johnson that something had to be done right away. So a memo was distributed to all home office supervisors, outlining the proposed changes and progress to date. Each supervisor was asked to pass along the information to his or her people.

The memo recommended that employees be assured there would not be a reduction in workforce, although the conversion would result in some job changes. Supervisors were asked to tell everyone that comments or suggestions were welcomed.

When word was passed along, morale shot up immediately. The changeover was carried out six months later with no major problems.

Analysis

Johnson's overcautious attitude led him to believe mistakenly that secrecy was the safest policy. But, as a result of being kept in the dark, employees began fearing the worst. Wild rumors began to circulate, leading to a serious morale problem. The rumors were not put to rest until the facts were put on the table.

In Your Job...

1. Do you keep more secrets than you should? ___Y ___N

2. Do rumors ever circulate because of secrecy in your unit? ___Y ___N

   Is secrecy hurting you? Explain:

3. Do you pass along to your people all the legitimate news you can? ___Y ___N

4. Note below any recent news you have not passed along.

5. Do you make yourself available to talk with people about things that may be upsetting them? ___Y ___N

6. What could you do to keep your people better informed?

Keep in mind that it's not always enough to inform individuals. How you inform them plays an important part in how well the information is received. From time to time we need to evaluate our communication effectiveness – both in transmitting and in receiving ideas, feelings and information. Lloyd was successful by writing and circulating a memo.

In what instances are you successful? With whom? In which areas? Why? What you can we learn from these successes for improvement in other situations? What are your areas for improvement? With whom? On what subjects?

Managing is a series of transactions between individuals. The success of these transactions depends on how well individuals understand each other. We are heavily dependent on what others do for us, and unless we understand each other it is difficult to obtain the cooperation so essential for accomplishment and progress. Things get done because people cooperate with one another to achieve desired objectives through meaningful and timely communication.

The most powerful communication tool is not what we say or write, but what we do. It is not what others are told but what they accept and believe. People can do almost anything if they want to do it, are trained to do it and understand the reason for doing it.

Using the list on the next page, rate the effectiveness of your communication, then consider how you would be rated by your boss, by your subordinates and by your associates. For each of the 18 items write the name of the person within your organization with whom you communicate most effectively. Then, for each of the 18 areas list the name of the person with whom you could most improve your communication effectiveness.

Are You Communicating as Effectively as You Could?

1. **Good news** — recognizing accomplishment, achievement, advancement etc.
   Best: _____   Worst: _____

2. **Bad news** — reporting progress less than expected, missed promises, unacceptable quality and other disappointing results.
   Best: _____   Worst: _____

3. **Plans** — explaining future and projected activities both short-term and long-term.
   Best: _____   Worst: _____

4. **Policies** — interpreting important guides to action and commitments concerning relationships, actions and responsibilities.
   Best: _____   Worst: _____

5. **Changes** — modifying assignments, schedules, priorities, dates, standards, procedures.
   Best: _____   Worst: _____

6. **Rumors** — handling unofficial and unconfirmed feelings, hopes, fears and predictions.
   Best: _____   Worst: _____

7. **What is expected** — letting others know what they are supposed to make happen; setting objectives for quantity, quality, service and cost; imparting bases for judgment of performance.
   Best: _____   Worst: _____

8. **How are we doing** — recognizing results currently and periodically in comparison with planned objectives.
   Best: _____   Worst: _____

9. **How can we improve results** — getting commitment for planned improvement in accomplishment, achievement and innovation.
   Best: _____   Worst: _____

10. **Listening** — hearing, giving attention to and understanding others.
    Best: _____   Worst: _____

11. **Directions** — instructing others day-to-day on what is to be done, when, why and how.
    Best: _____   Worst: _____

12. **Questions** — asking and encouraging others to ask, about uncertainties, interests, problems and difficulties; answering inquiries.
    Best: _____   Worst: _____

13. **Complaints** — receiving and considering expressions of dissatisfaction, discontent, uneasiness and resentment.
    Best: _____   Worst: _____

14. **Suggestions** — receiving and showing consideration of ideas for improvement.
    Best: _____   Worst: _____

15. **Approachability** — availability when others need to communicate with you.
    Best: _____   Worst: _____

16. **Timing** — imparting information at appropriate time for desired results — neither too soon nor too late.
    Best: _____   Worst: _____

17. **Objectivity** — reporting factually without bias or prejudice and with due regard to personal feelings.
    Best: _____   Worst: _____

18. **Selling ideas** — persuading and convincing others to accept suggestions and to take appropriate action.
    Best: _____   Worst: _____

The payoff of this exercise will depend on your:

1. Recognizing your need to improve your communication effectiveness.
2. Identifying a few specific areas and subjects where you need to improve and can improve.
3. Identifying the persons with whom you communicate effectively and those with whom you need to do better.
4. Planning your individual program and committing yourself to putting it into effect.
5. Measuring the results and continuing your development as a communicator and manager.

Your Communication Effectiveness

How effective are you in communicating within your organization? Rate yourself (0 to 100; 60 is passing) on each of the 18 areas. Then enter for each of the 18 items how you think (a) your boss, (b) your subordinates and (c) your associates would rate your communication.

	Rating of Self	Your Communications Rating		
		(a) Boss	(b) Subor.	(c) Assoc.
1. Good news	____	____	____	____
2. Bad news	____	____	____	____
3. Plans	____	____	____	____
4. Policies	____	____	____	____
5. Changes	____	____	____	____
6. Rumors	____	____	____	____
7. What is expected	____	____	____	____
8. How are we doing	____	____	____	____
9. How can we improve	____	____	____	____
10. Listening	____	____	____	____
11. Directions	____	____	____	____
12. Questions	____	____	____	____
13. Complaints	____	____	____	____
14. Suggestions	____	____	____	____
15. Approachability	____	____	____	____
16. Timing	____	____	____	____
17. Objectivity	____	____	____	____
18. Selling ideas	____	____	____	____
TOTALS	____	____	____	____

How to Interpret Your Communication Effectiveness Rating

In a study of 1,000 managers' ratings of themselves, Professor Earl Brooks at Cornell University discovered the following median ratings:

	Median Percentage
Overall Effectiveness as Communicator	81%

Effectiveness in Communicating:

1. Good news	* 84%
2. Bad news	71
3. Plans	70
4. Policies	67
5. Changes	76
6. Rumors	68
7. What is expected	74
8. How are we doing	76
9. How can we improve	73
10. Listening	* 83
11. Directions	* 85
12. Questions	79
13. Complaints	74
14. Suggestions	78
15. Approachability	* 85
16. Timing	74
17. Objectivity	* 83
18. Selling ideas	78

* Rated higher than the median.

It is noteworthy that:

- Self-ratings were lower than the median overall rating on 13 of the 18 items.

In general, the managers in this study believed that:

- Their bosses would rate them higher than their own rating.
- Their subordinates would rate them lower than their own rating.
- Their associates would rate them about the same as their own rating.

Now compare your self-rating with the rating you gave for your boss, each of your subordinates and each associate selected. Discuss with each of them the areas where improved communication is needed most.

Compare Your Results

Questions for Communication

Now that you have a feel for how effectively you communicate in certain areas, let's get down to specifics. Think of the last one-on-one conversation you had with a subordinate or peer. If the discussion could have gone better, and if there were any unexpected reactions, ask yourself the following questions:

1. What was the purpose of the meeting?

2. Did I give this person a chance? Did I pay close attention to what he or she said — or did I tune him or her out after a certain point?

3. Did I assume that this person had nothing new to tell me?

4. Is there an area of agreement that I overlooked?

5. Did I judge what the person said — or what he or she looked like?

6. Did I react to any statements he or she made?

7. Did I look for the middle ground in the issue? Or did I take an "either-or" position?

8. Did I take too much for granted? Did I check my assumptions against the facts?

9. How do my assumptions check out with the facts?

10. Was I objective? Or was I going on preconceived notions?

Think of your answers to these questions. The one factor they all have in common is whether or not you LISTEN.

The next time you must communicate with someone, stop and think. Then respond.

Failing to Listen Has Risks

One-half of the total communication process is listening. Most people are convinced they're good listeners. It would be wonderful if this were true. But the sad fact is, most of us do a lousy job of listening. This point has been proved in numerous studies that reveal we absorb only about 30 percent of what we hear. And this low percentage figure occurs when conditions for listening are just about perfect.

When the environment is less than ideal, the rate of listening efficiency tumbles to disastrous levels. When you fail to listen, you risk:

- Misreading people's intentions

- Misinterpreting ideas

- Confusing the issue

- Misjudging people's qualifications

- Getting instructions wrong

- Jumping to wrong conclusions

- Antagonizing people

Have you ever wondered just how good a listener you are? Being a good listener is not just resisting the impulse to interrupt a speaker. It is much more complicated. A conscious effort must be made!

> *"Silence is never more golden than when you hold it long enough to get all the facts before you speak."*

> *"I was on the way to the doctor with rear-end trouble when my universal joint gave way, causing me to have an accident."*
> *Collected Collisions from the Toronto Sun*

How Well Do You Listen?

How well do you listen? While the value of good communication is widely recognized, the emphasis is often on the giving end. But receiving — listening — is just as important. The following questions were prepared to help you discover how well you listen. Try to answer each question honestly and objectively. Then score yourself and see where there is still some room for improvement.

The Listening Quiz

When taking part in an interview, discussion or group conference, do you:

Usually Sometimes Seldom

1. Prepare yourself physically by facing the speaker and making sure that you can hear?   ___ ___ ___

2. Watch the speaker as well as listen to him or her?   ___ ___ ___

3. Decide from the speaker's appearance and delivery whether what he or she has to say is worthwhile?   ___ ___ ___

4. Listen primarily for ideas and underlying feelings?   ___ ___ ___

5. Determine your own bias, if any, and try to allow for it?   ___ ___ ___

6. Keep your mind on what the speaker is saying?   ___ ___ ___

7. Interrupt immediately if you hear a statement you feel is wrong?   ___ ___ ___

8. Make sure before answering that you've taken in the other person's point of view?   ___ ___ ___

9. Try to have the last word?   ___ ___ ___

10. Make a conscious effort to evaluate the logic and credibility of what you hear?   ___ ___ ___

See page 220 for scoring instructions.

If you didn't score as well as you might have, these insights will be worth your earnest consideration. Watch for clues to help you in specific areas.

Listening Techniques

A. Objectives in Listening

The objectives when we listen to people are basic and simple.

1. We want people to talk freely and frankly.
2. We want them to cover matters and problems that are important to them.
3. We want them to furnish as much information as they can.
4. We want them to get greater insight and understanding of their problems as they talk it out.
5. We want them to try to see the causes and reasons for their problems.

B. Some Do's and Don'ts of Listening

1. In listening we should try to do the following:
   - Show interest.
   - Be understanding of the other person.
   - Express empathy.
   - Single out the problem if there is one.
   - Listen for causes to the problem.
   - Help the speaker associate the problem with the cause.
   - Encourage the speaker to develop competence and motivation to solve his or her own problems.
   - Cultivate the ability to be silent. Successful people usually know how to remain silent.

> *"The person who listens consistently with understanding is the one who is most likely to be listened to."*

2. In listening, don't do the following:
   - Argue.
   - Interrupt.
   - Pass judgment too quickly or in advance.
   - Give advice unless it's required.
   - Jump to conclusions.
   - Let the speaker's sentiments too directly act on your own.

C. Complexity of People and Situations and the Need for Good Listeners

1. We think we understand people and all the difficulties involved, when frequently we don't even listen to them.

2. We think we understand a situation when we see only part of it and experience even less.

3. We think we understand the problems people face when we may have only a surface acquaintance with their elements and relevance; in actuality, we may be dealing merely with symptoms, not causes.

4. We should realize that listening is a key to knowing and understanding.

   - One way to know more is to listen more and to get more information.

   - A person's judgments and decisions are only as good as the information upon which they are based.

   - We need to discard the "allness" orientation, namely, that we know or have all the answers. We can never know all about anything.

   - We need to approach people and their problems with greater humility and recognition of the complexities involved.

   - We need to listen with greater intensity.

   - We need to observe with greater acuity.

   - We need to react to other people with greater empathy.

   - We need to synthesize what others say, think and feel with greater understanding.

"At home, he never stops talking."

Anne Marceau, wife of mime Marcel Marceau

The truth is that listening is one of the best methods for transmitting important feelings and attitudes. The way you listen can tell a speaker many things:

- I think that what you believe is important.

- I am interested in you as a person.

- Although I am 100 percent in disagreement with your position, I know that it is valid to you.

- I'm not trying to judge or evaluate you as a person, I just want to understand you better.

- You are worth listening to, and I am the kind of person with whom you can talk freely.

As is true of all behavior, listening is contagious, whether between two people or among a large group of people. But to ensure good communication, one must first take the responsibility for establishing reliable listening patterns. The person who listens consistently with understanding is one who is eventually most likely to be listened to.

Those who invest the time and effort necessary for improving their personal listening skills not only experience an increase in their effectiveness, they also upgrade the quality of their relationships with family and business acquaintances. These skills are reflected in the use of the techniques listed on page 212 as originally developed by Dr. Robert Burns, founder of Science Research Associates and the Industrial Relations Center at the University of Chicago. Memorize them. They will serve you well!

> *"...listening is hard work, requiring a heavy output of energy. Those who do listen effectively experience an increased heartbeat, faster circulation of blood, and even a rise in body temperature."*

5 Listening Techniques

TYPE	PURPOSE	EXAMPLES
Clarifying	1. To get at additional facts. 2. To help the person explore all sides of a problem.	1. "Can you clarify this?" 2. "Do you mean this...?" 3. "Is this the problem as you see it now?"
Restatement	1. To check meaning and interpretation with the other person. 2. To show you are listening and that you understand what is being said. 3. To encourage the speaker to analyze other aspects of the matter being considered and to discuss it with you.	1. "As I understand it then, your plan is..." 2. "This is what you have decided to do and the reasons are..." 3. "I see. Then how do feel about..."
Neutral	1. To convey that you are interested in listening. 2. To encourage the person to continue talking.	1. "I see." 2. "Uh-huh." 3. "That's very interesting." 4. "I understand."
Reflective	1. To show that you understand how the person feels about what he or she is saying. 2. To help the person to evaluate and temper his or her own feelings as expressed by someone else.	1. "You feel that..." 2. "It was a shocking thing as you saw it." 3. "You felt you didn't get a fair shake."
Summarizing	1. To bring all the discussion into focus in terms of a summary. 2. To serve as a springboard for further discussion on new aspect or problem.	1. "These are the key ideas you have expressed..." 2. "If I understand how you feel about the situation..."

You are Listening Poorly When...

- You are so busy framing your reply that your thinking gets in the way of your seeing and hearing.

- You feel dull and bored, unable to attend to each word.

- You are willing to dismiss the communicator as "unimportant" because he or she can't hurt or help you.

You are Listening Well When...

- You are able to repeat back what has just been said to you.

- You see the body language that goes with the verbal message.

- You aren't embarrassed to ask for a moment to think when you have been too busy listening to frame your reply.

- You habitually find value in every person who seeks to communicate with you.

"Nature has given to men one tongue, but two ears, that we may hear from others twice as much as we speak." Epictetus

You're aware of the need for good listening, but how about the importance of questioning? Through good questioning, more information may be obtained and the door to effective communication may be opened. There is no wrong or "dumb" question, except the one that isn't asked.

In dealing with the performance of subordinates, asking the right questions of the subordinate (in terms of what the job requires) is a basic need for development and an important skill of the administrator.

Questioning Techniques

The power of the question lies in the fact that it compels an answer. If we ask the right questions, we will get the right answers — in terms of information, experience, reactions or other data that we seek. If we ask the wrong questions, we will get the wrong answers.

Asking has many advantages over telling. In the first place, for managers to manage effectively, they must have adequate information. Indeed, people's decisions are only as good as their information.

Managers can never know as much about certain problems as their subordinates. If they try to make decisions concerning subordinates without sufficient and adequate information, they will make poor decisions and lose the respect and willing cooperation of their subordinates. There is no way a manager can gather certain kinds of information without doing a good job of questioning.

The higher people advance in the management hierarchy, the more they are removed from the points where actual work is performed. Consequently, they must rely more and more on written communication — reports, memoranda and the like, as well as oral communication. The quality and adequacy of the communication from others depend to a large degree on the effectiveness of the questions directed to them.

In using questioning methods, it is important that the user have a positive attitude towards the importance of asking rather than telling and equally important, a conviction that people, because of their unique experience, background and training, can potentially contribute unique information. With this basic attitude and conviction, the next need is:

a. To understand the different types of questions — their nature, purpose and use.

b. To understand the direction of questions — how to channel and handle them.

c. To develop skill and proficiency in using questioning techniques in appropriate situations.

On the following pages the basic types of questions are shown along with examples. Use each of them often and you will soon find that you are asking these types of questions without even thinking about it.

Types of Questions

Factual

The pupose of a factual question is:
1. To get at additional facts.
2. To open discussion.
   Examples:
   • What, where, why, when, who and how?

> *"In any discussion, stress the affirmative aspects of the situation. This means being positive and constructive."*

> **Factual Questions**

Explanatory

The purpose of an explanatory question is:
1. To get reasons and explanations.
2. To broaden discussion.
3. To develop additional information.

Examples:
- "In what way would this help solve the problem?"
- "What other aspects of this should be considered?"
- "Just how would this be done?"

Justifying

The purpose of a justifying question is:
1. To challenge old ideas.
2. To develop new ideas.
3. To get reasoning and proof.

Examples:
- "Why do you think so?"
- "How do you know?"
- "What evidence do you have?"

Leading

The purpose of a leading question is:
1. To introduce a new idea.
2. To advance a suggestion of your own or others.

Examples:
- "Should we consider this as a possible solution?"
- "Would this be a feasible alternative?"

Hypothetical

The purpose of a hypothetical question is:
1. To develop new ideas.
2. To suggest another, possibly unpopular opinion.
3. To change the course of the discussion.

Examples:
- "Suppose we did it this way. What would happen?"
- "Another company does this... Is this feasible here?"

Alternative

The purpose of an alternative question is:
1. To make decisions between alternatives.
2. To get agreement.

Examples:
- "Which one of these solutions is best, A or B?"
- "Does this represent our choice in preference to...?"

Coordinating

The purpose of a coordinating question is:
1. To develop consensus.
2. To get agreement.
3. To take action.

Examples:
- "Can we conclude that this is the next step?"
- "Is there general agreement then on this plan?"

Explanatory Questions

Justifying Questions

Leading Questions

Hypothetical Questions

Alternative Questions

Coordinating Questions

Ask the Right Questions

There is an increasing need for better information. Yet, we are bombarded with messages from morning until night, and the subject matter is more and more complex.

Our communication is not precise, and neither is our language. Much of both is crammed with unneeded information. Talk is cheap, so we spend it recklessly.

The best way to get at specific facts and feelings is to ask the right questions, such as:

Facts/Feelings	Questions
1. To identify and isolate	**What** happened?
2. To differentiate and separate	**Which** one did you choose?
3. To locate and specify	**Where** does this belong?
4. To single out individuals, groups, organizations	**Whom** do you mean?
5. To specify date and time (calendar and clock)	**When** did you return?
6. To get at reasons, causes and explanations	**Why** do you believe that?
7. To quantify and measure	**How** much was involved?
	How many did you see?
	How soon will you know?
8. To encourage suggestions and action	**How** do you think we should react?

"In archaeology you uncover the unknown. In diplomacy you uncover the known."
Thomas Pickering, U.S. Ambassador to Israel

Dependence on verbal communication or memory is often inadequate. Do not overlook the...

Reasons for Putting It in Writing

Should I Put It In Writing?

— To remind or refresh your memory.

— To allow time to reread, absorb, consider and appraise facts or ideas.

— To document occurrences and develop guidelines for future planning.

— To assure accuracy of records.

— To give or receive orders or instructions.

— To prepare reports.

— To clarify thinking.

— To prevent misunderstandings.

— To save time.

— To plan ahead.

— To organize.

— To state an agreement or to confirm one.

— To keep lists of facts, addresses, dates, figures, etc.

— To keep track of what has been read or said.

Remember, the preferred way of clarifying specific information is to put it in writing. For example, in our earlier case study when Lloyd Johnson put his company's plan in writing, rumors stopped and morale improved.

"Millions of dollars worth of valuable ideas have been lost because of the want of a stub pencil and a scrap of paper."
Alex Osborn

Summary:

In addition to the other benefits discussed in this chapter, a final benefit of effective communication is that rumors can be avoided. When you communicate effectively, people won't need to spend their time second-guessing. Nearly all organizations have "grapevines" for rumors. This informal communication method is often inaccurate and usually not trustworthy. Most often, rumors are destructive rather than productive. Rumors run rampant, especially when there has been no effective communication. Instead, communication ensures that people are aware of key issues affecting them and their jobs so they can keep their minds on productive, positive topics.

How to Stop Rumors

1. Realize that people are going to think and talk about things that affect them and their jobs.

2. Avoid a secretive attitude — "hush-hush" items are more interesting.

3. Decide if it is really important and possible to keep a particular secret.

4. Give people legitimate work-related news to talk about—plans and operations.

5. Don't keep anything "quiet" without good, valid reasons. Think more than once about those reasons.

6. Put the facts on the table promptly — available to everyone. Communicate!

7. Don't avoid confrontation indefinitely.

Questions for Personal Development

1. What is the major emphasis of this chapter?

2. What do you feel are the most important things you learned from this chapter?

   1)

   2)

   3)

3. How can you apply what you learned to your current job?

   1)

   2)

   3)

4. What objectives will you set to improve? By when (date)?

   1)

   2)

   3)

5. Who can help you most in applying what you learned in this chapter?

6. What are the major roadblocks you expect that may hinder your progress in applying what you learned in this chapter?
   Roadblock   **Why?**

   1)

   2)

   3)

7. How will you communicate the most important points in this chapter to your key people?

8. What preparation is necessary for this introduction?

?

9. What changes do you expect to make that will achieve greater motivation of your team?

Change   **By when (date)?**

1)

2)

3)

10. How will you monitor to assure that performance has improved, i.e., productivity has increased? (Reports, meetings, etc.)

11. What work-related problems concern you most in evaluating how you will benefit from this chapter?

12. Once you've accomplished several milestones, how will you continue developing new ideas and objectives related to this chapter?

13. How would you summarize the change you expect to see in yourself one year from now as a result of what you learned in this chapter?

SCORE YOURSELF ON THE LISTENING QUIZ:

On questions 1,2,4,5,6,8, & 10 give yourself:

10 pts for each answer of USUALLY
5 pts for each answer of SOMETIMES
0 pts for each answer of SELDOM

On questions 3,7,& 9 give yourself:

10 pts for each answer of SELDOM
5 pts for each answer of SOMETIMES
0 pts for each answer of USUALLY

If your score is:

90+   You're a very good listener.

75-89   Not bad, but you could improve.

74 or less   You definitely need to work on your listening skills.

*C*HAPTER 10

Problem-Solving

Problem-solving goals address areas that presently fall below the accepted norm or standard. Leaders are constantly looking for the problem areas so they can be taken care of before they get out of hand, before a crisis arises.

To be more effective managers tomorrow, we need to be able to handle today's problems. As we bring ourselves out of hesitation and indecisiveness in meeting our routine responsibilities, we are freed to solve problems and can then go on to plan constructively for the future.

The role of problem-solving was considered in Chapter 4 under the titles of "Goals on Your Job," "How to Think About Job-Related Goals" and "Categories and Classes of Goals."

Problem-solving objectives will always concern key result areas over which you have responsibility and for which you are accountable. To identify them, you might complete the following sentence: "I am dissatisfied with the current level of_____."

Why the Need for Problem-Solving

Perhaps:
- Performance has fallen off.
- You just have a feeling of uneasiness.
- A recent report (or a question from a superior) has brought something to your attention.
- One key result area on your list jumps out at you because you spend so little or so much time in that area.

The first step to resolving a problem is to recognize and isolate its key elements. This can best be done in two stages. Steps 1-6 on the facing page reveal the most likely causes and 7-10 determine solutions and action plans.

Problem-Solving Steps

Determining the Cause

The following steps will show you how to separate, identify and work through a problem:

1. **Make a brief statement of the problem**. This should be no longer than two sentences. For example, "I am dissatisfied with the current level of _____

   _____."
   Take only five minutes to do this.

2. **What is the present unsatisfactory level,** perhaps the status or measure of the condition in question? Find out the facts of the matter.

3. **What would be a reasonable desired level?** What would be acceptable performance?

4. **How did you arrive at the estimate of "desired" level?** (Industry norms, professional standards, previous achievement.) Be realistic.

5. **What are some of the possible causes** contributing to this unsatisfactory level of operation? (Brainstorm — come up with a long list.)

6. **Of those causes, which ones are the most likely causes?**

> *"The worst form of employee dishonesty is... to allow the boss to make a mistake that you could have prevented."*

Finding a Solution

7. **What are some of the alternative solutions** or proposed courses of action? (Brainstorm again — list ideas without evaluating.)

8. **What criteria for evaluating** are you suggesting as helpful among the alternatives? Possibly:

   - Contribution to objective — how much will this course of action contribute to arriving at the desired level?

   - Cost — net impact on financial position after costs are balanced by improvement in the result area.

   - Feasibility — physical ability to implement the course of action, considering company policy, other consequences.

   - Time involved.

   - Impact on morale.

9. **Fill in the score for each option** or possible alternative.

10. **Based on the discipline of the system,** what course of action is called for to solve this problem? Which alternative (or combination of alternatives) is most likely the best solution?

"No one would ever have crossed the ocean if he could have gotten off the ship in a storm."
Charles F. Kettering, one of the founders of General Motors

Performance-Based Management will be used as the framework for our problem-solving. Study the following example, and then use the worksheet for your problem, following these steps.

Taking Action

Write out a Time and Action Plan

Problem-Solving Worksheet (Example)

1. **Statement of Problem**
   I am dissatisfied with the current level of retail receivables in our division.

2. **Present Level**
   47 days of sales outstanding.

3. **Reasonable Desired Level**
   42-40 days of sales outstanding.

4. **Basis for Estimate of Desired Level**
   Previous historical data.
   Impact on profit position.

5. **Possible Causes**
   Attitude of retail manager — considers it low priority.
   Lack of knowledge of tools to handle this area.
   Systems-flow problems.
   Inadequate staff.
   Policies administered inconsistently.
   Location and size of operation.

6. **Most Likely Causes**
   Attitude of retail manager — considers it low priority.
   Systems-flow problems.

7. **Alternative Solutions** (Options)
8. **Criteria for Evaluating** (Contribution/cost/feasibility)
9. **Time and Action Plan** (Who will do what by when)

   Examples:
   Garden Division will adopt control system within 90 days.
   Jim T. will include article on receivables in each monthly edition of dealer magazine for next 12 months.
   Tom W. will send 10 worst offenders to appropriate management course within 3 months.
   Lisa M. will bring in new Receivables Manager from Garden Division within 30 days.
   James O. will add another clerical position in the department by 5/15.

Problem-Solving Assignment

Now that you are familiar with the process, let's look at one of your area's real problems. Select a problem that you have recently been struggling with. Using your solution(s), add target dates for beginning, completing and evaluating the action. Include specifics and various steps or phases. Work through the outlined steps with your problem in the space provided.

Problem-Solving Worksheet

1. **Statement of Problem**

2. **Present Level**

3. **Reasonable Desired Level**

4. **Basis for Estimate of Desired Level**

5. **Possible Causes**

6. **Most Likely Causes**

7. **Alternative Solutions** (Optional)

8. **Criteria for Evaluation** (Contribution/ cost /feasibility)

9. **Time and Action Plan** (Who will do what by when)

> *"No problem can stand the assault of sustained thinking."*
> Voltaire

Try this process once more with the following case study, "The Mysterious Problem." You will find that a variety of problems can be analyzed in this way — personnel-related issues as well as operational/organizational ones.

"The Mysterious Problem"

Kate Tyrone, a supervisor at Twining Fabrics, is up against a problem that is more personal than professional. The problem is Dale Rogers, one of her subordinates. It isn't that there's anything wrong with Dale's performance. On the contrary, her work is always of high quality. It's for a different reason that Kate is worried.

Dale has always been known as cheerful and chatty around Twining. Everyone likes her, and she's respected for her professionalism. She's a glutton for work — perhaps to excess. As a supervisor, Kate feels she has no reason to be concerned.

But that doesn't mean Kate has been unaware that Dale hasn't been her old self for the last six months. She's still the star of the department and still gives more hours to the job than anyone but Kate herself. But there's something wrong. Dale doesn't seem happy. She isn't as sociable as she used to be, and Kate has noted a cynical turn creeping into the jokes she makes.

Perhaps the strongest evidence of something being wrong is Dale's rate of absence. In the past she was virtually never out a day from the job, but in the last few months she's missed six days with stomach problems and severe headaches. There's nothing out of line in Dale's attendance record; after all, Twining allows its employees ten sick days every year. But being sick is not like Dale, and that has Kate worried.

It happens that, as supervisor and subordinate, Kate and Dale are friendly without being friends. Kate is uncomfortable about asking Dale if something is wrong, and in respect for Dale's privacy she has not asked questions. However, she has discussed the change in Dale with some of Dale's peers, and they can't account for the change in her behavior either. "I asked her once if something was wrong," said Barry Richards, "but she just said 'I've got something on my mind.'"

Kate dropped in on Dale this morning on a business matter. She surprised Dale staring at the wall with a look of such sadness on her face that it shakes Kate to remember it. "Everything OK?" she said to Dale. "Uh-huh," Dale replied. Kate got the information she needed and left.

Kate has had that scene on her mind all day. She knows that something serious is troubling Dale, but she does not want to overstep her role as supervisor and intrude in an employee's personal affairs. But her conscience nags her. "What am I supposed to do?" she asks herself.

Questions

Does Kate have any professional interest in Dale's apparent troubles?

"Idealism increases in direct proportion to one's distance from the problem."
John Galsworthy

If Kate does decide to intercede, how should she go about it?

Are there any reasons why Kate should not let Dale work out her problems by herself?

Some problems seem to remain in an organization when they should have been worked through. Here are some of the main reasons. Check those that apply to your situation now.

Self-Analysis: Why Problems Aren't Solved

> *"Experience is the name everyone gives to their mistakes."*
> Oscar Wilde

	Applicable to My Situation Now	
	Yes	No
• Subordinates often will not criticize supervisors.	___	___
• People tend to be protective of their positions and hopes for promotion.	___	___
• The presence of people with technical expertise tends to intimidate those who are afraid of admitting ignorance.	___	___
• A sense of urgency tends to stimulate unreliable judgments.	___	___
• Personal conflicts often work against cooperative problem-solving.	___	___
• People see problems from their own viewpoint, rather than from a broader organizational perspective.	___	___
• Focusing on a distasteful situation clouds the atmosphere with tension, fear and uncertainty for both parties.	___	___

What other lingering problems do you face? Can you identify any of the reasons for them? Are there any additional reasons? If so, add them to your list.

If you answered yes to any of these reasons, you have to move through four basic steps to a decision:

1. Analyze the problem.
2. Find alternative solutions.
3. Analyze and compare alternatives.
4. Choose best alternative.

Another key reason that often occurs in the workplace is that many individuals are hesitant, even afraid, to make decisions. Decision-making is important to every manager. Although there is risk involved, there is even greater risk in complacency or procrastination.

Decision-making is the end result of problem-solving.

> *"My decision is maybe — and that's final."*

> *"The only people who can justify thinking more about yesterday than tomorrow are historians."*

Decision-Making Process Chart

Graphically, the decision-making process looks like this:

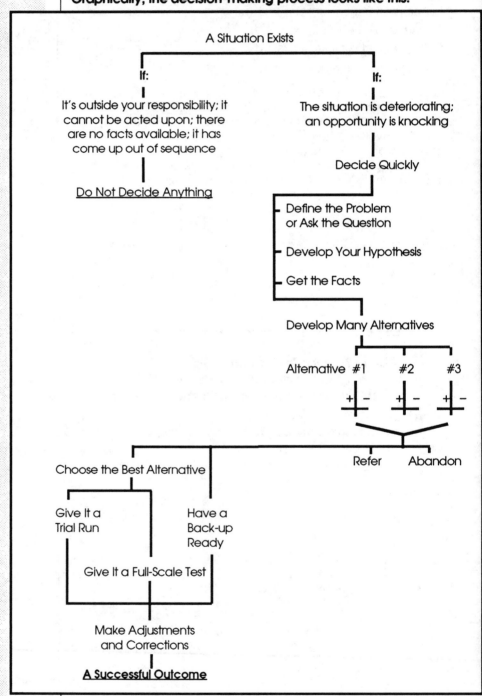

Worksheet: Decision-Making Process

To gain added facility in decision-making, use the worksheet below and fill in the specifics of a decision you're working on right now. This will help you focus your energies, find weak spots in your decision and come up with the best possible alternative.

The situation is:

The facts are:

The alternatives I see are:

The best alternative I believe is:

The action steps to be taken are:

The "bottom line" results I expect are:

"If at first you don't succeed, try, try again... then give up. There's no use being a damn fool about it."
W. C. Fields

Summary:
Present or Future Thrust?

Problem-solving and decision-making skills must be applied to both current and future issues.

A basic question for all managers is: "How can I maintain an acceptable level of performance on current operations and still anticipate future problems?" Realize that there are differences in emphasis that must be understood.

> *"Author Alex Haley keeps two old sardine cans and 18 cents framed in his home as reminders of a time when that was all he had in the world."*

Daily Operations Involve:	Future Planning Involves:
Unit goals related to organizational goals.	Strategy and new goals.
Previous experience as a base.	New variables.
Functional and professional perspective (means).	Overall significance (ends).
Relatively short-term evidence of results.	Long-term consequences.
Tangible incentives to improve.	Incentives diminishing with gradual change.
Repetition, familiarity, confidence, security.	Fewer guidelines, risk, trade-offs, wider margin of error.
Benefits quite obvious.	Benefits uncertain, usually postponable.

By utilizing the steps learned in this chapter, both present and future problems can be resolved. If you decide to use these methods regularly you will soon be surprised by the improvement in your decisions. Decide to be a problem-solver today.

Questions for Personal Development

1. What is the major emphasis of this chapter?

2. What do you feel is the most important thing you learned from this chapter?

   1)

   2)

   3)

3. How can you apply what you learned to your current job?

   1)

   2)

   3)

4. What objectives will you set to improve? By when (date)?

   1)

   2)

   3)

5. Who can help you most in applying what you learned in this chapter?

6. What are the major roadblocks you expect that may hinder your progress in applying what you learned in this chapter?

   Roadblock   **Why?**

   1)

   2)

   3)

255

7. How will you communicate the most important points in this chapter to your key people?

8. What preparation is necessary for this introduction?

9. What changes do you expect to make that will achieve greater motivation of your team?

Change   **By when (date)?**

1)

2)

3)

10. How will you monitor to assure that performance has improved, i.e., productivity has increased? (Reports, meetings, etc.)

11. What work-related problems concern you most in evaluating how you will benefit from this chapter?

12. Once you've accomplished several milestones, how will you continue developing new ideas and objectives related to this chapter?

13. How would you summarize the change you expect to see in yourself one year from now as a result of what you learned in this chapter?

 CHAPTER 11

Developing New Ideas

The family had recently moved to town. They overslept one morning and the seven-year-old son missed his school bus. The mother, though late for a meeting, agreed to drive him if he would direct her.

They rode several blocks before he told her to turn the first time, several more before he indicated another turn. This went on for 25 minutes — yet, when they finally reached the school, it proved to be only a short distance from their home.

Asked why he had led the mother over such a round-about route, the child explained, "That's the way the school bus goes, and it's the only way I know."

How often do you overlook a "better way" in favor of the "way it has always been done"? How do people come up with new, innovative ideas?

Eight Steps to New Ideas

Have you concluded that creative managers have some secret source of ideas? Do you think they have some special gift that you don't have?

Actually, everyone has the ability to originate ideas and solve problems. The process is rather simple. It is based on the way our minds combine ideas to create new ones.

Problem solutions and new ideas are created by changing old ideas or experiences, by processing or manipulating them. We combine them in new ways, put them in a new context of time or place, add other ideas, take something away, or change their meaning or purpose. We may do this accidentally and unconsciously, or we may do it deliberately and consciously.

The question is, how do we go about this in a systematic and fruitful manner? What is the process of working with experience to produce new ideas or to solve new problems?

Here are eight suggested steps:

1. **Name the target.** What's the problem? What kind of idea do you need?

2. **Get the facts.** Pile up all the information you can about the problem. This should include unsuccessful attempts to solve it. Often ideas that failed one time will, with a slight change, succeed at another time.

3. **Try the obvious solutions first.** Often merely naming a problem and collecting data about it will suggest solutions.

4. **Next: Try the wild ideas.** In particular, look for the apparently trivial, irrelevant aspects of the problem.

5. **Think intensely about the problem.** This is not really a separate step, but part of the steps we've mentioned before. Make yourself think about the problem until you have a solution or until you've reached what might be called a state of frustration.

6. **Walk away from the problem.** Put it out of your conscious mind. At this point, if you have covered steps one through five, your subconscious will usually take over.

> *"Do not follow where the path may lead. Go instead where there is no path and leave a trail."*

7. **Seize the flash of insight.** Generally, at some indefinite time after you walk away from the problem, you will find an answer welling up in your mind. Seize the idea at that moment and get it on paper.

8. **Do something about the idea.** And above all, don't give up. We tend to get discouraged too easily. There are really easy ways to have good ideas, to solve tough problems. In the pursuit of an idea, the odds are all in favor of running into periods of discouragement when nothing goes right, when it appears that the answers will never come, when you begin to doubt the wisdom of what you are doing.

> *"People can alter their lives by altering their attitudes."*
> William James

History is full of people who, through sheer determination, hung on through such periods — the Wright brothers, Alexander Bell, Morse, Edison. In my books, *Nobody Gets Rich Working for Somebody Else* (Dodd Mead, 1986) and *How to Take the Advantage: Lessons from America's New Breed of Successful Entrepreneurs* (Scott, Foresman, 1987), I summarize the results of over 400 cases of living Americans. One of my most significant conclusions is that anyone who wants to try something new must go through disappointment and times when it seems much wiser to give up.

Developing Innovative Objectives

It seems natural to think of innovations when considering goals. To help clarify innovative goals, let's begin by reviewing our definition of the other two job-related goals. The distinguishing feature of a **routine goal** is that it is repetitive. It concerns result areas that are ongoing, where the output is achieved over and over again. The commitment contained in the routine goal statement is simply a description of the standards or levels of performance considered par for the course. **Problem-oriented objectives** deal with those result areas where present performance levels fall below the accepted norm. The commitment you seek in this goal statement is to arrive at a solution.

What is an innovative goal? It deals with a third type of result. Innovative goals deal with changes, with new things, with risk, with different outputs, either because they are being sought for the first time or because they are unique, one-shot affairs. You will know you're in the innovative area whenever your initial thoughts about the objective make use of words like *develop, initiate, inaugurate, implement, begin, design, create, study, rewrite, reorganize, rearrange, "re-"* almost anything.

Innovative goals are the opposite of routine goals because they are not expected to be repetitive. They are sometimes suggested by problem situations, since they sometimes make a contribution to remedying unsatisfactory performance, but they are distinct in that they should describe new results.

When negotiating these goals, up and down, it is desirable that the commitment be not only to develop, begin, study, etc., but to accomplish something as a result of what you develop, begin, study, etc. We don't seek change for the sake of change, but to bring about some payoff or benefits.

What are the distinguishing features of innovative goals? Change and risk with significant added benefits, if successful.

Format for Innovative Goals

The recommended format for innovative goals includes four items that should be included in an innovative goal statement: Ideas, Results, Method and Timetable. Each of the four items requires full consideration and negotiation.

1. Ideas

Write your own innovative idea on the following *Innovative Goal Worksheet.* These questions might help: "What new idea do you plan to install, suggest, develop, study, etc., in your area of authority during the next operational period? What new project do you have in mind that goes beyond the repetitive operations of your work unit"?

> *"The people who get on in this world are the people who get up and look for the circumstances they want, and, if they can't find them, make them."*
> George Bernard Shaw

Notice that this is not the goal. This is only the innovative idea you have. This is the brainchild you gave birth to when thinking about your responsibilities. This is the name of the project you have in mind. This is the creative thought that crossed your mind as you were driving to work, or that you thought of while eating breakfast this morning, or that woke you up like a light going on in the middle of the night.

2. Results

The actual goal, the output, is the desired improvement that set you thinking. What is the payoff you expect? What are the concrete improvements/benefits that you think warrant the expenditure of time, money and energy involved in the new idea? Outputs are the only justification for spending the organization's resources. Outputs are the only way to determine whether programs (routine or innovative ideas) are successful and deserve to be continued. We might think a program is worthwhile, but we'll know only if the innovation produces the desired results. It is possible to introduce the innovation, succeed in making the change, but fail in producing the results expected and therefore fail in achieving the goal.

3. and 4. Method and Timetable

To achieve any benefits, there are always certain associated costs. Every innovative goal statement is a small cost-benefits comparison. You may think the benefits are worthwhile, but only worth a limited investment of the unit's resources. The question you have to ask: "How much are we willing to spend on these benefits?" You may not be better off achieving the results if the costs are too high.

Costs are itemized under the words "Method" and "Timetable." Costs include not just dollars, but all resources that might be spent — time costs, energy costs, people costs, opportunity costs, frustration costs — all costs expended to achieve the intended results. After the initial costs, how about maintenance costs, policing costs, abandonment costs (if necessary later). Nothing is worth more than you are willing to pay for it. Maybe you can't afford it, nice as it might sound.

> *"There is one thing stronger than all the armies in the world, and that is an idea whose time has come."*
> Victor Hugo

Method should include all the steps that will be necessary to implement and track the innovation — actions and expenditures listed step-by-step. Beside each item in this list, under the word "Timetable," a time period or completion date should be listed. A simple completion date for the whole project is not enough if objectives are supposed to provide a way to monitor progress throughout the period.

"Rule of Success: Trust only those who stand to lose as much as you when things go wrong."

It is important to know when to abandon projects. Many times what seems like a good idea turns out to be unworkable for some reason. We have to know when things outlive their usefulness or when they never do live up to their promise. Even if the results are achieved, it is possible that the idea will fail because the costs are too high. Costs should be reviewed on a fairly regular basis in case they begin to outweigh the advantages.

Remember to differentiate between the idea and the goal. For example: Suppose you have been concerned about declining sales in a given territory. After much discussion, you decide it is a good idea to try direct mail advertising. Is your goal to mail advertisements? No. That is the idea. The goal is to increase sales. You can succeed in completing the advertising program but fail because sales remain the same.

If you haven't completed your *Innovative Goal Worksheet* step-by-step as you were reading, go ahead and complete it now.

Innovative Idea Worksheet

1. Innovative Idea: _____

_____

_____

_____

_____

2. Desired Results: _____

_____

_____

_____

3. Method: _____   4. Timetable: _____

_____   _____

_____   _____

_____   _____

_____   _____

_____   _____

_____   _____

_____   _____

_____   _____

Ask each of your subordinates to complete an *Innovative Idea Worksheet* for an idea of his or her own. You may be pleasantly surprised by your subordinates' creativity and the potential impact of their ideas.

The following case study, "Why Change?," shows how sharing innovations and planning with subordinates' does not eliminate obstacles due to the human factors involved.

"Why Change?"

When Barbara was promoted to supervisor and moved to the claims department of an insurance company, she was viewed with suspicion by the men and women in her new department. Because Barbara was soundly grounded in the clerical procedures used there, she believed there were many improvements that could be made. Not wanting to give the impression of being too eager, however, Barbara spent the first week or two just getting to know the people in her department. On the whole, the staff was pretty standoffish. This was especially true of Jack, one of the older claims analysts. On the bright side, Barbara was able to make friends with Tony, one of the sharp new clerks.

One of the costly practices Barbara noticed was that the claims form was initially posted to a logbook by a clerk, then given a preliminary classification by an analyst before being returned to the clerk for detailed verification of the data on the form. After this, the form went back to an analyst for completion. Barbara reasoned that the clerk who entered the form in the logbook could be trained to make the preliminary classification. The same clerk could also verify the detailed data on the form. This way, unnecessary doubling back of the form would be eliminated, and the analysts could spend more of their time on the complex aspects of claims processing.

Barbara waited until Friday and then proposed to the clerks and analysts that on Monday the new procedure should be followed. She demonstrated to all the clerks how the classifications could be made with the same master list used by the analysts. Since there were no objections and only a few questions, Barbara presumed that the work group understood the new procedure.

C A S E   S T U D Y

On Monday Barbara made a point of working along with Tony because he was the newest clerk in the office. He easily caught on to the new way. Tony seemed sold on the improvement, and by noon he had finished as much work as he normally would have before the additional step was added to the job. That afternoon, however, Tony reported to Barbara that he had run into all sorts of difficulty in following the new procedure. The next morning Barbara discovered that Tony was back to doing the job in the old way. Barbara checked the rest of the staff and found that no one other than Tony had even given the new method a try. In fact, when she queried Jack about it, Jack said this was an old idea that had been tried before and found to be full of problems. Barbara then went back to Tony and suggested he try a variation whereby his problems with the new method might be worked out. Tony shook his head and said, "This is not as good an idea as it looked at first. If it were, other people in the department besides me would be trying it. Anyway, I would rather follow the old procedure. It's much simpler."

Questions

1. Why do you suppose Tony gave up on the new procedure so soon?

2. How might Jack's reaction have influenced the other employees?

3. Should Barbara persist in trying to install the new procedure? Why?

4. How might Barbara have gotten her innovation accepted in the first place?

C A S E   S T U D Y

Ideas Must Yield Results

Barbara's ideas were sound. But her methods of implementation did not produce the desired results.

Listed below are possible results of innovative ideas. Remember, even the best ideas must be "sold." Others must understand the benefits and want to achieve them.

INNOVATIVE IDEA	RESULTS
Reorganize the department	equitable workload; enlarge span of control
Conduct a feasibility study	potential income; potential monitoring
Install a new service	at what cost; criteria of success
Automate an operation	save money, people; add information
Research a community service	need to be met; cost/benefit
Design a new procedure	time- or cost-saving; with what specs?
Replace a machine	quantity, quality, cost
Conduct a survey	of whom? on what?
Forecast something	accuracy; timeliness
Prepare a report	completeness; acceptability w/o rewrite
Present new education program	documented shortage/need; public impact

Now let's try another case study.

First, review the example below. It illustrates clearly the four elements required to prepare innovative goals:

- Background
- Objective
- Method and Timetable
- Results expected

Next, read the case study on pages 246 and 247, then complete the brief worksheet on page 248 on an innovative idea of your own. Be creative! Don't be inhibited by the past. Personnel issues (problems) may set the tone for a whole work group. Your innovative approach in solving them will greatly enhance your overall effectiveness. (This particular case also reviews many topics from previous chapters.)

Example of an Innovative Type of Objective

Project Records Supervisor

Background Facts:

The Project Record dictations are getting increasingly difficult to transcribe, because:

- the engineers are not speaking distinctly.
- they are not indicating at the start of a second belt for the same project that this is a continuation of the same.
- the various subheadings of the report (completion schedule, past history, etc.) are not stated, but are left for transcriber to figure out.
- project numbers are frequently omitted.
- important dates are frequently omitted.
- last names of some key managers are difficult to understand and should be spelled out.

Objective:

- To reduce our two-week backlog of untranscribed and half-complete (because unintelligible) dictations to two days.

Method and Timetable:

- Meet with Project Director (responsible for those doing most of this dictation) within 15 days.

- Arrange for demonstration of dictation equipment by salesperson in order to train users on dictating techniques. 30 days.

- In case of unintelligible words or mix-ups, place belt in engineer's folder, so he must listen to own dictation and make corrections.

- Report to be given to Project Director each week of all files not corrected in 48 hours.

Results Expected:

- Reduction in backlog from two weeks to one week within six months.

- Reduction in backlog from two weeks to two days within twelve months.

"The Constant Complainer"

Ruth Smyth was the best all-around clerk that Gibraltar Finance Company's data processing section ever had. She was a natural for being promoted to supervisor when the time came. During Ruth's first few weeks as section supervisor, everything went well. She obviously knew the work flow from A to Z. Given this chance, she quickly cleared long-standing bottlenecks and eliminated a number of duplications. Her experience and good judgment easily won the respect of the people who worked for her. On the other hand, Ruth was a stern and serious taskmaster. She was fair and courteous with her employees, but she showed little interest in them beyond their ability to get the work done.

As Ruth settled into the job, however, she had an uneasy feeling that something wasn't quite right in her section. Her employees came to depend on her decisions in the slightest matters. If a problem arose, they were likely to sit at their machines waiting for orders from Ruth. At first Ruth felt flattered by this dependence. But this caused her work load to gradually build. Increasingly, she found herself giving curt instructions and short answers to people in her work group.

One employee in particular, Woodie Beck, a keypunch operator, really irritated her. Regardless of what the assignment was, he found some fault with it. Additionally, Woodie

C
A
S
E

S
T
U
D
Y

regularly complained about his terminal, his chair, the lighting, the temperature or his co-workers. Ruth responded to each of Woodie's complaints and requests with some attempt to accommodate him or to set the problem straight.

To make matters worse, the quality of Woodie's work, which had otherwise been unspectacular but acceptable, began to fall off. He made errors. Frequently his tapes had to be checked and re-keyed. When this continued, Ruth called Woodie into her office. "I've been very patient with your unending complaints and requests," Ruth said, "but lately your work has been far below what is considered satisfactory. If it continues, I'm going to recommend that you be suspended or discharged."

"I'm sorry about my work," said Woodie. "I've had all kinds of problems at home. My oldest son was expelled from high school for drug dealing a couple of months ago. Neither my wife nor I can seem to keep him out of trouble anymore. It's driving us both crazy."

"Family troubles are a bother, I know," said Ruth, "but you can't let them interfere with your work. What's important right now to you is the fact that the quality of your work is no longer acceptable. If it continues, you will lose your job. My advice to you is to find some way to keep your concerns about your son from affecting your work. Otherwise, your problems will be even worse. I've been very fair with you, but you owe your first attention now to improving your work. Unless it improves, I'll have to put you on notice."

Questions

1. What are Ruth's strengths and weaknesses as a supervisor?
2. How well do you think Ruth handled the problem with Woodie's work? What was good and what was bad about her approach? What do you expect will be the results of Ruth's conference with Woodie?
3. If you were Ruth, how would you have handled Woodie's problem?
4. What suggestions/innovations can you make to Ruth in order for her to improve the quality of her supervision?
5. What suggestions/innovations can you make to Ruth in order for her to improve the quality of Woodie's work and eliminate his constant complaining?

CASE STUDY

Photocopy this page and analyze a problem
you have, generating new ideas.

Personal Innovative Goal Worksheet

BACKGROUND FACTS: _____
_____
_____
_____

OBJECTIVE: _____
_____
_____
_____

1. Innovative Idea: _____
_____
_____
_____
_____

2. Desired Results: _____
_____
_____
_____

3. Method: _____   4. Timetable: _____
_____   _____
_____   _____
_____   _____
_____   _____
_____   _____

Questions for Personal Development

1. What is the major emphasis of this chapter?

2. What do you feel are the most important things you learned from this chapter?

1)

2)

3)

3. How can you apply what you learned to your current job?

1)

2)

3)

4. What objectives will you set to improve? By when (date)?

1)

2)

3)

5. Who can help you most in applying what you learned in this chapter?

6. What are the major roadblocks you expect that may hinder your progress in applying what you learned in this chapter?

Roadblock   **Why?**

1)

2)

3)

7. How will you communicate the most important points in this chapter to your key people?

8. What preparation is necessary for this introduction?

9. What changes do you expect to make that will achieve greater motivation of your team?

Change   **By when (date)?**

1)

2)

3)

10. How will you monitor to assure that performance has improved, i.e., productivity has increased? (Reports, meetings, etc.)

11. What work-related problems concern you most in evaluating how you will benefit from this chapter?

12. Once you've accomplished several milestones, how will you continue developing new ideas and objectives related to this chapter?

13. How would you summarize the change you expect to see in yourself one year from now as a result of what you learned in this chapter?

*C*HAPTER 12

Managing Your Career

Now that you're familiar with how to develop new ideas, let's take the concept one step further by applying it to career management.

You already know that developing new ideas involves looking for a better way to accomplish goals and that means change. Career management involves looking at what's working in your career development strategy and what's not. It involves finding new approaches for solving what can sometimes feel like impossible challenges.

Career management begins with you — not your teacher or even your employer. This chapter starts with a discussion of the question, "Are you managing your career or leaving it to chance?" It continues by describing 10 steps to successful career management, five skills to help you advance in your chosen career and three essential management areas to be mastered.

Are You Truly Managing Your Career or Leaving It to Chance?

Career: one's progress through life or in a particular vocation; a profession or occupation which one trains for and pursues as a life work.
Webster's New World Dictionary

A group of five professionals ranging in age from 30 to 50 was talking with Jennifer, a career development counselor. They were discussing what they liked and didn't like about their jobs and careers, about what they wanted to do in the future and why they seemed to be "getting nowhere fast." To help create forward career movement, Jennifer said, "Tell me how you got the position you now hold." Their answers were diverse.

Sandy said, "The position opened up. I applied for it because it was exactly what I thought my next logical career move should be, and I got the job — just as I'd gotten every earlier promotion I'd applied for. That was six years ago; since then, I've been overlooked for two other promotions. It's like my career has come to a dead end. I was on a very fast track, being promoted every two or three years, until now."

Job: a specific piece of work, as in one's trade, or done by agreement for pay; anything one has to do — task, chore, duty; a position of employment; situation; work.
Webster's New World Dictionary

Jeff said, "Your experience is just like mine except for one difference. My company wants me to accept another promotion, and I'm trying to find the courage to turn it down. It's not that I don't want it, it's that I suddenly realize that my kids are growing up fast. I want to go to their soccer games, track meets and school plays. I want to be involved in their lives. I'm tired of being an absent dad. If I take this promotion, I won't have time for my kids. But if I don't take it and it is the perfect next step for me, I'm afraid I'll ruin any chance of reaching the top in my profession."

Kelly said, "My company saw skills in me I didn't and approached me about the position. I said 'yes' because I saw it as an opportunity. I've more than met the challenge, and they are pleased with my results. While I love this company and don't want to leave, I'm getting bored. I keep hoping they will suggest another opportunity for me, but so far they haven't."

Randy said, "My last employer eliminated my position due to budgetary problems and down-sizing. I was unemployed and looking for the right job, but time and money ran out before the right job came along. This company made me an offer, and I took it even though it wasn't my first choice. You have to pay your bills, you know. I try to give the job my best efforts, but it's hard when you don't really like what you do. My boss just told me I'd better shape up or I'm out the door. I don't want to get fired, but I think I'm about to be."

And Jeanne said, "On a fluke. I took a job with this company because I needed a second job to make ends meet, and this organization offered the only night job I could find that paid decent money and didn't involve telemarketing, selling insurance or waiting tables. The next thing I knew, I was working here full-time, and last year they made me a manager. I'm very happy. But, there's a conflict inside of me that I can't resolve. One part of me doesn't feel any desire to do anything else because this job allows me to use all my best skills and brings a new challenge every day. Another part of me feels guilty because there is probably something better out there."

As you can see from these examples, there are many issues involved in career management and different routes people travel to find jobs. Some approaches are more proactive than others. All may work fine — up to a point. However, in each case a point was reached where the issue became who was managing whom — was the career managing the person or was the person managing the career?

Just as each of these professionals got their jobs by following a different career management approach, each now faces a different career management challenge. How they choose to face and resolve it will determine if they are truly in charge or if they allow circumstances to control themselves.

> *"We are not interested in the possibilities of defeat."*
> Queen Victoria

> *"Courage is the price that life exacts for granting peace."*
> Amelia Earhart

Remember, to avoid failure is to limit accomplishment; avoiding failure is not the same as success.

When you paddle your own canoe, you can do the steering.

Sandy's approach was highly structured and planned. He knew what he wanted, what it would take to get it and carefully pursued and accepted opportunities that took him in the direction he wanted to go. But, he ran into a wall that made him feel like his career had dead-ended before he reached his ultimate career goal. So, Sandy's challenge is to figure out how to create new options and forward movement.

Jeff's approach was also very deliberate. Like Sandy, Jeff knew exactly what he wanted, what it would take to reach the top of his profession and carefully pursued and accepted opportunities for forward movement — until now. Suddenly, Jeff finds himself questioning what's really more important in life — being an active, hands-on dad or reaching the top of his profession. In short, his career goals have collided with his family and personal goals. Jeff's challenge is to figure out how to be at peace with himself. This may require that one goal be put on the back burner so the other can thrive.

Kelly's approach was more reactive. It involved saying "yes" or "no" to a new option presented to her and accepting or rejecting an opportunity that offered the chance to use skills she didn't know she had. Now, she's ready for another career move. Her challenge is to stop hoping and to start doing — to change from a reactive approach to career management (waiting for the company to offer another opportunity) to a proactive approach (seeking a new opportunity).

Randy tried to hold out as long as he could afford to be unemployed until the perfect job presented itself. Finally he had to make a difficult choice — accepting a less than perfect job offer or facing financial devastation. He chose the job. But now, he's not performing as expected. His challenge is to make an important decision — to treat what he knows is a temporary job just like it was his chosen life's work. Once that decision is made, it will be easier to motivate himself to be a productive employee, even though he dislikes his job (he owes himself and his employer that much), while he pursues options that are better suited to his skills and interests.

Jeanne's method involved deciding what type of work she was willing to do and how much she wanted to earn in a second job to help make ends meet. Because of what she calls a "fluke," she found her career company, her career position and her life's work. Jeanne's challenge is to realize that it's okay to be happy and content with your job, to stop feeling guilty about being happy and to avoid complacency by forming a back-up plan just in case she ever needs one.

Identify Your Special Challenge

How did you get the position you now hold? Did you actively seek it? Did it seek and find you? Did you get it on a fluke? What career management challenge are you facing now? The clearer you are about the career management approach you've been following and what it is you are trying to resolve, the easier it will be to uncover the options that will help you choose the best next step for you.

Career Strategy #1

Your career management approach: How did you get the job you now hold? _____

_____

_____

_____

_____

_____

_____

_____

_____

Your career management challenge: Describe what you're trying to resolve or answer about where you are and/or where you want to be. _____

_____

_____

_____

_____

_____

_____

_____

Now study the 10 steps to successful career management that follow, and select the step — or steps — that will help you resolve your challenge; use the form beginning on page 298 to plan your strategy for putting that step — or steps — into effect.

10 Steps to Successful Career Management

Step One: Be a Self-Starter — It's Your Career

Staying proactive means relating your career plan to the challenges you're facing now.

Taking control of your career means first having the courage to acknowledge you have hopes and then finding the courage to pursue them. It's the only way to truly make a career plan your own. Once you have a plan, you'll be able to move toward accomplishing it.

When you run into a roadblock or obstacle as you pursue your dream, take a proactive approach. Rather than saying or thinking, "There's nothing I can do," ask or think, "Is my career/life dream still important enough for me to find the energy and time to overcome this roadblock?" If the answer is "yes," then identify all the ways you can resolve the roadblock. After you know your options, choose the one that appears to have the best chance of helping you attain your goal. If the answer is "no," identify what your new dream/goal is and how you will go about reaching it.

The remaining nine steps are all part of a proactive approach to career management. While it is difficult to plan for every eventuality, it is possible to have basic strategies for handling unexpected challenges that come your way. The best time to plan for the unexpected is before something happens, because after it happens, we're often too shocked, emotional, angry or devastated to think clearly.

> *"If a man advances confidently in the direction of his dreams to live the life he has imagined, he will meet with a success unexpected."*
> Henry David Thoreau

> *"Change is the price of survival."*
> Gary Player

Step Two: Plan for "What Ifs"

The goal of planning for "what ifs" is to help you understand that your future depends on the decisions you make today.

Planning also helps you avoid becoming complacent or hesitant. Considering "what ifs" makes you more sensitive to the signs that a "what if" is about to happen and prepares you to take positive action when it does.

For instance, before we accept a position that we think will be wonderful, we should ask, "What if I'm wrong? What if I hate it when I get there?" We make the commitment ahead of time that regardless of what happens, we'll stay a productive employee, give it a fair chance and then look for a better match. When we feel that the job we hold is one we would never choose to leave, ask, "What if I'm forced to change even if I don't want to?" We can reassure ourselves that, even though it's not pleasant, we do have choices, and we will survive unexpected change.

We tend to avoid planning for the "what ifs" because they often represent our worst fears, and most of us approach fears by ignoring them and hoping they'll go away. Yet, fears rarely leave on their own.

One of the best ways of taming a fear is to define it, face it head-on and develop a strategy for handling it.

"Long-range planning does not deal with future decisions, but with the future of present decisions."
Peter Drucker

Step Three: Give Your Best Effort Every Day

When we control what is within our power, the things beyond our control are easier to accept and manage. The choice of whether or not to give our best effort every day is completely within our control.

You owe it to yourself and to your employer to put forth your best effort, no matter what is occurring in your environment. If you are receiving a paycheck for a job, you are expected to perform. Not giving your best effort is the same as quitting without leaving. When we quit without leaving, we lose self-restraint. We also give control of the choice to leave or stay to our employer, because when we don't perform, he or she has the right to ask us to leave. If we are asked to leave before we're ready, we usually feel even worse about ourselves. It can be an endless cycle, but one we can completely control.

Step Four: Determine What You Do Best and Do It

Whether you do what you love for full-time pay, part-time pay or as a volunteer, there's always a way to bring what you love to do into your life work.

When you're doing what you love, your heart sings, your days are filled with purpose, you have more energy, and you're more fun to be with. If you love to do lots of things and aren't doing any of them regularly, pick one, identify all the ways you can do more of that one thing and then choose the way that best fits your schedule and lifestyle. Focusing will keep you from becoming overwhelmed — the biggest killer of initiative.

> *When we control what we can control, other things are easier to accept and manage effectively. That's why it's important to give our best efforts every day — the choice to do so or not is completely within our control.*

> *Life is a continuous process of getting used to things we never expected.*

Step Five: Only You Can Decide

Successful career management means constantly responding to changing work environments. Nothing remains constant — especially during tough economic times. That's why identifying your special career management problem is so important. You can't solve a problem you haven't identified. Once you know what you're dealing with, you can define your options and make the best decision possible at the time.

Remember, not deciding lets someone else control your destiny. Sometimes people hate to make decisions because they're afraid of being wrong. When we make decisions, we either get the desired outcome or we do not. Either way, the results are opportunities to make future decisions that either move us toward our objective or improve our situation. Seeing results as opportunities for further action is the mental shift you must make.

Step Six: See Yourself as Others See You

When we can step out of ourselves long enough to see our situation through the eyes of others, choices previously hidden often become clear.

For example, if you don't like your job and feel unmotivated to perform at a level of excellence, try looking at how your behavior is creating problems for your co-workers. It may not make you like your job any better, but it may help you find that motivation to change your actions so you stop punishing others for your dissatisfaction.

Step Seven: Remember It's okay to Be Happy with What You Have

In our society, where better is often defined as "more," it's easy to get caught up in feeling that what we have is never enough.

So, if the job you hold enriches your life, perhaps it's time to recognize that you've won the career race. Pat yourself on the back — you've achieved a goal most everyone else is still striving for!

Step Eight: Give Yourself Permission to Change

Change is really a matter of being willing to let go of rigid thinking patterns or habits that keep us from finding ways around roadblocks. It is dangerous to keep wishing things could be as they were one or two or 20 years ago.

If you eliminate the "C" and the "E" from the word CHANGE, you're left with the word "hang." Many industries are undergoing tremendous changes; people are expected to meet the challenge of change by learning and then applying skills they never thought they'd need. If we resist change, we put the noose around our own necks and "hang" ourselves. Refusing to change limits our options for career success. Deciding to change is proactive because the act of changing is the one quality that keeps us vital.

> *"The trouble with the rat race is that even if you win, you're still a rat."*
> Lilly Tomlin

> *"When you're through changing, you're through."*
> Bruce Barton

283

Step Nine: Define Yourself by Who You Are, Not by What You Do

When we define ourselves by what we do rather than by who we are, we set ourselves up for a major fall. If what we do is suddenly taken away (we're fired or laid-off or passed over for a promotion, etc.), finding a new job takes a back seat to finding ourselves and that prolongs the job hunt.

Remember, what we do is an important part of who we are, but it should not become the whole. A profession is part of our exterior image like clothing. So, if you haven't already done so, take time to discover who you are on the inside. Once you know the inner you, you'll be able to survive any experience.

Step Ten: Aim for Balance

The most successful and happiest people have clear goals for all parts of their lives, not just their careers. In addition to your career goals, set family goals, financial goals, personal goals and spiritual goals to help you bring balance and contentment to your life. Achieving balance can be difficult, but it can be done — especially if you prioritize these goals in order of importance and then refer to your list before you make a major decision. For example, if you truly believe that your family comes first, choosing to put your time and energy into family time rather than into a new promotion will be an easier choice.

Now that you've studied the 10 steps for successful career management, use these suggestions to help you make the decisions that will help move you forward.

> *"Let the world know you are as you are, not as you think you should be, because sooner or later, if you are posing, you will forget the pose, and then where are you?"*
> Fanny Brice

Career Management Strategy #2

My career management challenge (from career management
suggestion #1):

_____

_____

_____

The step(s) that will help resolve my career management challenge is (are):	What I can do specifically to apply this step to create movement:
Step:	Step:
_____	_____
_____	_____
Step:	Step:
_____	_____
_____	_____
Step:	Step:
_____	_____
_____	_____

Focus on Skill Development to Advance Your Career

Successful career management means using certain skills. Other
chapters in this book focus on being performance-oriented rather
than task-oriented and how to clarify your mission, set goals, stay
organized and motivated and communicate well.

In addition to these important skills, let's look at five skills that
everyone needs no matter what his or her career choice.

Five Skills Everyone Needs

Skill #1: Selling Ideas and Negotiating for Results

Whether you're trying to convince your company to give you a raise, implement your innovative idea for solving a departmental or customer service problem or create a new position that allows you to help the company accomplish its important goals, sales and negotiation skills are critical to success. Yet, these are usually the last skills people think to develop — unless they've held positions in sales departments.

Selling and negotiating skills are really advanced methods of effective communication. You can have the best ideas in the world, but if you can't present them so others get excited enough to support them, your ideas remain just that — good ideas going nowhere. No matter what your position or career goals, you'll win more of what you want if you learn how to "sell" your ideas to others and to "negotiate" the details so everyone feels he or she has won. Use this career management suggestion to help plan a strategy for selling your ideas more effectively.

Career Movement Strategy #3

Identify Who You Need to Help You

The idea you want to "sell":

_____

_____

_____

The people who need to be excited about the idea if it is to be implemented:

_____

_____

_____

What you think the "hot button" (major reason for wanting to support the idea) for each person is:

_____

_____

_____

How each person will benefit (refer to "hot buttons") by supporting this idea:

_____

_____

_____

Now that you've done your homework, form your strategy for approaching these people. I suggest you begin by talking with the person you feel will be the hardest to convince. After all, if this person "buys in," the others are most likely to. Or, perhaps you'll talk first to the person you feel has the most influence on the "big resister" — sometimes support for your cause helps convince those who are most hesitant.

Skill #2: Thinking Before Doing

This may be the biggest challenge of all because performance-thinking is the opposite of what most of us were taught. Task-thinking is reactive — a problem arises or we see a need, so a task is created to solve the problem or meet the need.

In most businesses, task-thinking is the norm. One of the best examples on the corporate level is to look at how most organizations go about determining and making budget allocations. The executives tell department managers to project their budget needs for the coming year. This usually creates a frenzy of activity about how each department will get a maximum slice of the dollar pie. If dollars remain in the current year's coffer, managers go on a spending spree. After all, how can they get as much next year if they didn't spend what was allocated this year? This is the task-thinking approach to annual budgeting.

The performance-thinking approach looks much different. When budget time approaches, executives and managers get together to determine first what major goals must be accomplished during the next budget year if the company is to achieve its mission. Then they look at what it is going to take — time, money, people, other resources — to accomplish those goals. Then they look at how they need to allocate dollars to various departments to ensure that the company achieves its mission and goals.

With performance-thinking, departments aren't penalized or rewarded for how they spent last year's allocations because the focus isn't on what gets spent. It is on what needs to happen if the organization as a whole is to maintain its competitive edge in its industry.

Performance-thinking involves looking at issues in new ways — ways that most organizations are only beginning to address by focusing on quality management and implementing self-directed work teams.

On a smaller, more personal-performance scale, every minute of every day we choose whether to use performance-thinking or task-thinking to accomplish our goals. If we are in customer service and let the number of customers we talk with be our evaluation criteria, we are using task-thinking, not performance-thinking. If our goal is to help find the right solution to the problem for every customer we speak with, we are using performance-thinking. The difference, of course, is how we define success — in terms of numbers reached or results accomplished.

Skill #3: Finding a Mentor — and Becoming One Yourself

Most people who achieve their goals in the corporate environment will admit they didn't do it by themselves. They looked for people who had achieved similar goals or who exhibited certain important success qualities and made these people their mentors.

But, that's not all they did. They went one step farther than the average person. To keep from being pigeon-holed into a job with no way out, they also looked for someone to mentor. There's always someone who sees the job you have as being a wonderful next career step. The key is to find that person and help him or her develop the skills needed to take your place. It takes courage — especially if your biggest fear is that you'll put yourself out of work — but preparing someone to take your place motivates you to find a way to get out of your pigeon-hole and into a new career position.

Use this career movement suggestion to help you fine tune your performance-thinking skills.

> *Mentor: a wise, loyal advisor; a teacher or coach*
> Webster's New World Dictionary

> *Protégé: one who is protected or trained or whose career is furthered by a person of experience, prominence or influence.*
> Webster's Ninth New Collegiate Dictionary

Career Management Suggestion #4

Identify a Mentor and a Protégé

What are the qualities or skills you must learn to achieve your next career goal?

_____

_____

_____

_____

Identify potential people to mentor you: Who do you know that models these qualities or skills successfully?

_____

_____

_____

_____

Identify people whom you can mentor: Who would see your skills and qualities as being important to their success?

_____

_____

_____

_____

> *"The essential factor that lifts one man above his fellows in terms of achievement and success is his capacity for greater self-discipline."*
> Ray Kroc, founder of McDonald's

Skill #4: Becoming Self-Disciplined

No doubt about it. Successful career management takes a great deal of soul-searching, goal-setting and self-discipline because every day brings lots of diversions that can deflect us from our paths. The best way to become self-disciplined is to do it.

Skill #5: Determining Whether You Are Better at Building or Maintaining

If you're better at building, look for career opportunities where you can think of solutions, implement new ideas, establish new departments, take risks. If you're better at maintaining, look for opportunities that help you fine tune and maintain what someone else sets in place. Building and maintaining are very different roles. However, both are critical to every organization. Remember, builders need to be able to do some maintaining — and vice versa. The key is knowing which is your primary skill. When you do, you will proactively look for opportunities to use this skill in ways that will make you stand out and help your organization accomplish its mission faster.

Three Essential Management Areas to Be Mastered

"Workforce 2000" is a governmental study commissioned in 1989 to determine the answer to the question, "What does the workforce need to be able to do by the year 2000?" According to the study, managers need to develop three special competencies to be effective.

Skill #1: How to Manage Outside Resources

The study projected that by the year 1995 60 percent of all people who work in large corporations will be working not as paid, full-time employees who receive salaries and benefits, but as vendors who are contracted to provide a specific service within a specific time frame and at a fixed cost.

Because vendors have a lot to lose if they fail to meet the specifications of the project they were hired to do, companies feel they can be held more accountable than full-time employees. And, because vendors pay their own benefits, the dollar savings to most organizations can be substantial.

The challenges for managers, though, can be staggering. First, managers need to know how to clearly identify the goals of the project, define the task and measure the results vendors will be expected to create. Then, managers need to learn how to evaluate vendors (much like assessing candidates for a job) to ensure they contract with the right person or company. Next, managers need a higher level of knowledge about negotiating performance contracts with vendors. Finally, managers will be highly visible in the process of vendor selection. If they choose right, they will be heroes. If they choose wrong, they could be out of a job. In short, as vendor services become more of the norm in doing business, a manager's role will go through significant changes.

Skill #2: How to Manage Multiple Projects

Managing multiple projects is already a challenge. But as companies continue to down-size, combine two jobs into one and eliminate layers of management positions, the surviving managers will be expected to wear more hats, juggle more roles and ensure that more big projects get done right and on time. Process-management will become more important, and managers will need to make decisions about which projects or tasks have the greatest impact on the organization's mission and be sure that these projects are done first. Managers who approach multiple projects as a time management task will lose the battle. Managers who see this job as part of a process for accomplishing critical goals will win.

Skill #3: How to Use Computers and Software Programs

Knowing how to use computers is more than the ability to "hunt and peck" on a keyboard to type words on a screen. It means being able to do more of your own work, depending less on an administrative assistant and becoming knowledgeable about a variety of software programs that apply to your job and your industry. A good place to start, if computers are new to you, is concentrating on learning everything you can about the capabilities of the software programs your organization uses. Computers will become increasingly important to business by the year 2000. Today's proactive manager does whatever it takes to stay up to date with this important technology.

Summary

Effective career management requires a proactive rather than a reactive approach.

There are 10 steps to successful career management:

1. Be a self-starter.
2. Plan for the "what ifs."
3. Give your best effort every day.
4. Determine what you do best and do it.
5. Only you can decide.
6. See yourself as others see you.
7. It's okay to be happy with what you have.
8. Define yourself by who you are, not what you do.
9. Change before you have to.
10. Aim for balance.

Developing the following five skills will help you advance in whatever career you choose:

1. Selling ideas and negotiating for results
2. Thinking performance rather than task
3. Finding a mentor and becoming one yourself
4. Becoming self-disciplined
5. Knowing if you're better at building or maintaining

Three essential management areas to be mastered are:

1. How to manage outside resources
2. How to manage multiple projects
3. How to use computers and software programs

Remember, it's your career. The better your career management strategies, the more likely you are to get what you want out of working.

Questions For Personal Development

1. What is the major emphasis of this chapter?

2. What do you feel are the most important things you learned from this chapter?
    1)

    2)

    3)

3. How can you apply what you learned to your current job?
    1)

    2)

    3)

4. What objectives will you set to improve? By when (date)?

5. Who can help you most in applying what you learned in this chapter?

6. What are the major roadblocks you expect may hinder your progress in applying what you learned in this chapter?
    Roadblock   Why
    1)

    2)

    3)

7. How will you communicate the most important points in this chapter to your key people?

8. What preparation is necessary for this introduction?

9. What changes do you expect to make that will achieve greater motivation of your team?

     Change   By when (date)?
     1)

     2)

     3)

10. How will you ensure that performance has improved, e.g., productivity has increased? (Reports, indicators, measurements)

11. What work-related problems concern you involving this chapter?

12. Once you've achieved several milestones, how will you continue developing new ideas and objectives related to this chapter?

13. How would you summarize the change you expect to see in yourself one year from now as a result of what you learned in this chapter?

Closing Message to Managers

We have focused on you, as a unique individual. You as an employee. You as a leader in a supervisory role. Here is a summary of attributes of high performance in these roles that will serve you well.

Self-Esteem

You see yourself as valuable, worthy and capable. You know you can change and control the conditions that lead to your success.

Responsibility

You've put into motion the events that result in your successes and failures — and you acknowledge your accountability.

Optimism

There's every reason to expect that your future will be bright, good, productive and profitable.

Goal Orientation

You've learned to keep your goals before you continually, to live with them so that they motivate you and direct your behavior.

Imaginativeness

By habit, you can imaginatively experience new and beneficial situations before they happen.

Awareness

You are alert to what's going on around you and aware of new opportunities that can help you meet your goals.

Creativeness

You're certain there's a better way to do just about everything.

Communicativeness

You know that your success is largely rooted in your ability to get ideas across to others and to understand what others are saying to you.

Growth Orientation

You give high priority to the task of getting ready for your future. And you welcome the opportunity to trade old, unproductive habits for new, profitable thought patterns.

Positive Response to Pressure

You use pressure to trigger constructive responses so that you peak up — rather than cop out — when hostile conditions surround you.

Trust

You believe that people don't, as a rule, deliberately try to do badly, and you're comfortable tossing the ball to another member of the team.

Enthusiasm

Your energy is contagious. Others pick up your enthusiasm and begin to work with more enjoyment and involvement.

Risk-Taking

You are ready and willing to reach out and take reasonable risks. Your objective is excellence, not perfection.

Decisiveness

You make decisions now, and you take actions now— not because you have to, but because you want to. You reflect a sense of ability, forward motion, determination and accomplishment.

INDEX